I BLAME GOD

A Story Maneuvering my Personal Spiritual Journey

Author Desiree P. Middleton

Copyright © 2024 Author Desiree P. Middleton
All rights reserved.

ISBN: 9798880144242

TABLE OF CONTENTS

Acknowledgments

Preface

The Sunken Place

I'm Broken

Good Grief

Isolation

Say That Same Prayer

Put a Praise on It

Control the Trauma

If All Hearts Are Clear

I Feel It

Just a Little Talk

Renewed

Trust the Signs

It Ain't Over

I Still Blame God

I Blame God

ACKNOWLEDGEMENTS

This story is for all of us who have at one time or another, felt like we were forgotten. Those who felt like we were praying, and our prayers were continuously falling upon deaf ears. We were working hard, doing all that we could to stay afloat mentally, physically, spiritually, and financially, and nothing that we do or have done seems to work. We sit in the back shadows of rooms and watch while those who we feel may not be as deserving as ourselves flourish and seem to gain more blessings without fight or failure. While we, on the other hand, are in a daily battle for our lives, our sanity, and our spirituality.
God, don't you hear me? Can't you see me? Is this the life you choose for me? What have I done to deserve this?

This book is for those of us who don't understand the reasons for it all. We don't understand why our fight is so hard, why our mountains are so high, why our valleys are so low, and why our oceans are so wide. We feel as though we are often drowning in a sea of darkness, unable to kick our way back to the top as we gasp for air. This book is for those of us that have blamed God and meant it!

When I say that I blame God, I mean every ounce of the statement. No takebacks, no regrets and no refutes to what I say. I mean just that.

I hope that you can find inspiration within these pages, but not just inspiration to know that you are not alone in your thoughts, but also understanding, courage and strength... the strength necessary to continue to fight through your emotions, your doubts, and your circumstances. I fight with you; I cry with you, and I feel just like you. This book is for the US!

I also dedicate this book to my grandmother, the late Marguerite Young Smalls, with whom I received my introduction into the way and teachings of what it means to live holy. Also, to my mother, the Reverend Patricia Ann Smalls-Middleton, of the African Methodist Episcopal Church Doctrine of the Mighty Motivating Mount Pleasant District of the Palmetto Conference. Aa always, every book that I write, I dedicate to my daughter's, for you all are my reasons! To my Sunday school teacher, the late Mrs. Rebecca Chapman aka Miss. Sweet, and my YPD Church School advisor and cousin, Margie Steed, you all taught and gave me my foundation in my spiritual journey. Lastly, to my father, Kevin Wayne Middleton Sr., he was the one who taught me that loving God was not traditional, but personal. He showed me that it was okay to love God in my own way, as he demonstrated as uniquely as only, he could, in life and in death.
I love you all forever.

~ Author Desiree P. Middleton

PREFACE

A question that I have asked myself numerous times throughout this journey has been, how in the world did I end up here? How did I end up in such a deep and dark egregious depth of shallow thoughts, actions, associates, and impurities to where it attacked everything within me, around me, and connected to me? Me, being in an unhealthy version of myself, caused everything around me to be unhealthy. The more I fought to rid myself of the filth, the more it consumed me. I blamed God. The one omnipresent spirit that I knew could help me from all that I was drowning in, had seemed to be failing me before my very eyes. My prayers were going unanswered, my faith was rocky and my take on religion was becoming dim.

Helpless, hopeless, and afraid, I blamed God. I blamed God for it all because I didn't understand the who, the what, or the why. I was just living my life, as I thought I should. I was doing my darndest to raise my girls, I was working hard, I was not stealing, I wasn't scamming, or being fake with anyone around me, I wasn't sleeping with anyone's husband, I hadn't murdered anyone, I was not addicted to drugs or selling it, I was following the majority of the ten commandments, I was going to church, tithing a little bit, and I was helping others in whatever capacity that I could, genuinely with the little that I had. In my eyes, I was living right, or as best I could.

Why was I sinking? Why was life not flourishing for me? Why had God forgotten about me? He was the only one who could fix this, why wasn't he? Was he just going to allow me to be a failure and die right within these things that I was in? Who was going to care for my children if I couldn't? Why was God not coming to my rescue? Did he not hear the many prayers that I had been praying constantly on bent knees? Did he not care? I was confused. I was hurt. I had given up hope that he would rescue me. In my state of despair and turmoil, I had no one else to blame, so in a hasty decision, full of rage, I made my decision on who was at fault. I knew exactly who the culprit was and was hip to the shenanigans. My need for vengeance had consumed my immediate thoughts, and my tear-filled eyes had dealt with more than enough saturation to last many months. I knew who I was going to point the finger at, I knew who was behind my demise. I BLAME GOD!

THE SUNKEN PLACE

I still remember the day that I realized I had drowned, and that there was probably no resuscitation available that would give me the breath of air needed to continue life as it was in the state that I was in. I can still see myself, sprawled across the floor in my home office downstairs, screaming, hyperventilating, face wet with tears, and heart racing as if I had just run a marathon. It was around 5:00 in the morning, I was angry. I was depleted. I was heartbroken and I was rageful. It had only been a couple of weeks prior that I had packed all my husband's belongings and had them waiting for him outside of the back door when he arrived home. This marriage was taking every good thing that I had left in me. Trying to make it work to save us both, the embarrassment that eventually came anyway.

As I lay on that floor, I could not believe that I had found myself in this space once again. Separated for a second time, from a man I had intended to spend the remainder of my life with. An additional child to add, to what would be single motherhood again, when I had thought that chapter for me had finally ended. Oh, I was mad, very mad and hurt. How did God bring me here, to this sunken place, that I had fought so hard to get out of just a few years prior? Did he hate me so much that I was not even worthy of a successful and fulfilling companion in marriage?
I BLAME GOD!

I wanted it to work so badly that I ignored every obvious sign that had reared its ugly head in front of me. I dare not allow my society of peers to deem me incapable of "keeping a man." The constant scrutiny of others had sunken me into a pit of despondency that I was not willing to showcase in public view. I had given all that I had within me, and God had shown me no better. He had allowed me to get myself into this relationship, he had allowed this person to portray to me that he was godsent and tricked me into believing that this was a beneficial connection. God was the one that sent this demon in disguise to me, or allowed the enemy to, and wreak havoc on my mind, my body, my soul, and my faith. The only person that benefited from the ordeal was my soon-to-be ex-husband. Never had I imagined a man could become so mean, gnarly, vindictive, and sassy.

I had given everything that I had. A semi-healed heart, which was still healing from previous relationship traumas, a credit score that I had finally gotten to decent standards now in the mud once again because I felt it was my duty to help my man. My womb, I gave although I had publicly and very adamantly stated I was done having children. I gave me, all of me, to a man who did nothing but take, and never held the capability to replenish me in the places where I poured out to fill him because he too was empty, unbeknownst to himself or me.

I poured so much of myself into my marriage because I saw it as the blessing that God had sent me. An answered prayer, much like so many others. I thought that I had finally made it and that God was pleased with me. Little did I realize; he was probably more disappointed in me in this moment than any others from before.

Have you ever been in such despair that you found yourself

crying out aloud to the father, to just heal your heart, to just make it stop hurting? That was where I was on this day. It was not all about my marriage solely, but that was definitely the straw that broke the camel's back. It was the breaking point of many past traumas that I had yet to sit with myself or a therapist and deal with. I had mastered the art of covering up everything with smiles and a funny joke, and sometimes even alcohol, that when something traumatic occurred, it barely raised the hairs on my skin. Many people over the years have equated this to strength. Always telling me how strong I am, and how much resilience I have. If I had known better at that time, I would have very much taken those accolades as an insult. It certainly was not the badge of honor they had encouraged it to be.

It was instead a very unhealthy way to mask the things that would soon become boulders and chains tied to my feet to hold me down. The very same things that I made the decision to push way down into my subconscious and forget about, would be the same things that drowned me into an ocean so deep of what I would soon find out was going to kill me, literally, if I didn't choose to do things differently. It was this desperate cry for freedom from the bondage of my thoughts and my circumstances, it was this moment, on the floor in my office, it was this day, and this breaking point that was necessary to begin the work that would follow to help me rise from a very deep and dark sunken place.

Within this moment, I could hear my heart crumbling inside of my body like broken glass. God had forgotten about me! He had brought me to an unfamiliar place, dropped me off in the middle of nowhere and left me for dead. That was how I felt, and because my feelings in that moment outweighed my logic, my emotions were given permission to run amuck, bringing forth emotional and mental pain that I could feel in my body. My head hurt, my shoulders ached, my legs had no strength to stand and every joint in my body felt like ten-ton boulders were attached to them. This was what it was like hitting the bottom of a sunken place.

Imagine when a ship, like the Titanic, is unable to stay afloat in the ocean. It slowly takes in water and begins its journey to the bottom. That was my life for years, though I was unable to recognize it, I was sinking. Unable to patch the holes that had punctured my ship. Unable to rid my vessel of the onset of ocean water swallowing me whole. My ship slowly sank deeper and deeper, it became darker and darker until it finally hit bottom. Once it hit, everything broke apart. I was that broken vessel, and I had no idea how I was going to repair myself and rise back to the top. For me, I had felt like this was the end. I couldn't swim. No one could hear me down here. No one could see me. I had no emergency flares to shoot upward to gain anyone's attention. I was all by myself. Alone.

In this stillness, this dark room, just before the cracking of morning, I had cried all that I could, until there were no tears left to leave my eyes. I was shattered, but I was right where God wanted me to be. This was where he needed me to reside for a moment, to be able to recognize the path that I had led myself down. He needed me to be in a hopeless state, a state where I was not even able to recognize myself. A place so low, so cold and so despairing, that I would have a desperation for more, for better. In this sunken place is where I was going to find my victory. Of course, I did not know it then, but looking back on that moment, even now as I write these words, I can say, that was my turning point. It was the point of no return, I mean, where else could I go but upward? I was on the bottom; I couldn't go any lower. My life had plummeted, and I was yearning for better. This was the moment God probably smiled and said to himself, "Now she's ready!"

I had been doing things my way for so many years, I thought I was allowing God to lead, but in all honesty, I was the captain of this ship. He was probably more like the first-time cruiser that got seasick because I was hitting all the big waves causing the ship to bounce. Rock bottom was where he needed me to be so that he could gain control of the vessel and guide us back to the shore safely. The sunken place may have been my now, but it most certainly was not about to be my forever.

I'M BROKEN

The broken version of myself that came after that morning on my office floor provided me with a very despondent outlook on my life. I was going through the motion's day by day, but inside I was dead. I had lost all feelings and emotions, and my heart was shattered beyond repair. I was getting myself used to a new life with a baby, two adolescents and bills that exceeded what my pay could afford. My now estranged husband, bitter and lacking morale, made it extremely difficult to co-parent and settle our marital affairs. I too, bitter, and angry, did not let up on my demands. It was either going to be my way, or no way.

I began to realize very quickly how distant I was becoming from everyone, including my children that lived in the home with me. My baby girl, now only a few months past a year old, became the responsibility of her older siblings. When I arrived home from work, my regimen had become to shower and lay in bed with my phone mode turned to silent. I would order pizza or grab fast food on the way in so that the kids could have food, but other than assuring that they ate, I managed nothing else. Bills were beginning to consume my bank accounts, leaving me in the negatives until another bi-weekly payday arrived. My family and friends, unaware of the majority of what was happening in my household, only noticed my withdrawal, and settled on the cause being my busy schedule with work, and popular lemonade business developed along with my daughters, in which we named, Mani & Maya's Fruity Treats.
Depression and grief were taking total control of my

thoughts and protruded as actions. Even at my fulltime job, my previously overachieved work had now become bare minimum. I was using my PTO days more and more and had caught the attention of my supervisor enough for her to pull me aside one day to ask if everything was okay, as I was unlike my normal self. I masked the seriousness of what I had been dealing with and offered her nothing more than the explanation of my baby having been sick, and I was lacking sleep. This was not too far from the truth, as my daughter, having sickle cell, had been seen in and out of the hospital because of her condition during this time as well.

I had another traumatic experience to mask and bury deep down within the dark pit of my memory, another "thing" to not deal with. It was within this time that I had become the furthest from the grasp of God's hands than ever before. I purposely rejected him. The church that I was attending and beginning to grow within, had very abruptly become a breeding ground of the added dramatics of my failed marriage. I was far from feeling at all within the realms of the holy spirit, after all, God was to blame. It was the holy spirit that had failed me. In conversation with a friend, very heavily dropping my afflictions onto her, she asked "What has become of you?" in a very offensive and dry reply, I stated, "I'm broken."

Just as soon as I uttered the words from my mouth, the epiphany of my self-proclamation gave me an insightful vision into where I was, I was not just physically, emotionally, and romantically broken, I was spiritually broken. I was so broken that during this time, I felt I had forgotten how to even pray. I would fall on my knees in expectation of delivering proclamations of thanksgiving, receipt of blessings and guidance as I had done before when in prayer, only to utter nothing, or when I tried to speak, it sounded like gibberish. Even the unction to pray had left me, I was really alone. I was just flesh. It was these moments that I was unable to pray where I felt like God really did leave me and probably was ashamed of me for not following in his footsteps.

A girl that grew up in the church all my life, a preacher's kid, one who received the holy spirit at the age of thirteen, one who attended church regularly and could recite parts of the bible, had now been rejected by the very spirit she revered and praised for so many years.

It was this realization of loneliness that I began to turn away from the only religion that I had known. I felt that this could not have been a real thing if someone as humble and hardworking as myself was not even able to receive help from the spirits above, was God even real?
It was my own apprehension and confusion that wrestled me into an even deeper and much darker pit than the one that I was currently in.

To already be lost and feeling hopeless and to take God out of the equation was probably the most detrimental thing to my life that I could have ever done. I know that I am not the only one that had has ever felt like this, there may even be some of you feeling like this now. There was no one around me that could have helped me, this was a season of "alone" that I had to experience solely on my own. What I will offer to you if you are at this moment is something that I wish someone was able to give to me. God's promise, because regardless of what we are dealing with, or what we go

through in our lives, God has made us promises that he is always there, even when we cannot feel him, when we cannot see him, when we think he has gone away, he is always there. The evidence of this is in scripture, one that I would offer to you at this moment would be **Isaiah 43:2** "When you pass through the waters, I will be with you; and through the rivers, they shall not overwhelm you; when you walk through fire you shall not be burned, and the flame shall not consume you."
See, that's it right there, it is written in his words, right in the scripture! He is with us even in the storm, even in our brokenness, our sunken places, he is with us.

When I look back on that period of my life, as lonely as it had seemed, I still was not as alone as I thought that I was. The same creator who I had rejected, was still guiding me in a sense through the valley of despair that I had reached. I was never left alone, I look at it as the saying that my grandmother used to very frequently mimic towards her children and grandchildren, "God takes care of babies and fools.," I was the fool, because I was broken.

Logic had long left my thoughts. Causing me to voluntarily jump on a roller-coaster ride of emotions, thoughts, actions, and ailments. Lightly as we take it, when our minds and hearts are in disarray, our body follows. The broken pieces of ourselves are like sharp shards of glass that puncture and cause discord to everything attached to us, sometimes even bloodshed. Our children, our careers, our ethics, morals, friends, family, lovers, money, it all becomes affected when we are not in our best frame of mind. This lesson came to me in the hardest way possible, but as you will see as you continue to read, it was these many lessons that brought about major blessings.

The hurt that I was currently experiencing was self-inflicted unbeknownst to me. God had been trying to get my attention for many, many years. In my transparency and always having vowed to "Keep it real," I ignored the greater things that God was trying to do in my life, not wanting to become another act in the world of the new gospel that had now seemed to consume my generation. I did not want to be fake, I wanted to show others that were not one hundred percent convinced that God was real, that you could still be yourself, and serve God. I wanted my life to be a public view of what it meant to be honest with yourself and still love God.

There were many that had fallen astray because of the cinematic and theatrical genre that the new church had become. This wave of neon lights, two-steps, bunny hops down the aisle, hacks into the mics and fancy church attire had gained attention as trends, but when you would either witness or hear of these same actors being Godly on Sundays but living a totally different life Monday through Saturday, I too even questioned God within these moments. God... is this your child? Is this the person who you have chosen to be a representative of who you are to the lost sheep?

It was long after this question that I realized, our eyes must stay focused on our own plates. Depend on no one to show you who God is, that is a personal thing. You must know him for yourself. Receive guidance, but never dependance. I had still yet to reach the season to where that realization would come. There was much more work to be done before I would gain that insight. I was still in my broken place; I was still depressed and still in a season of hopelessness. Every day I awoke and monotonously garnished the same routine. Wake up, take the kids to school, go to work, come home, feed the kids, shower, go to bed. I had given up on prayer. I had given up on church. I had given up on having a relationship with God, to me, he wasn't real. It was at this time that I allowed my mind to become tainted with what religion really was. What was the truth and what was the lie?

I sought others who I knew did not share in the same traditional religion in which I had grown up on and questioned them about what they experienced and how they felt. I know that my grandmother turned over in her grave ten times. But I needed answers, and I wasn't receiving them from the God I had grown to love and worship. I researched and read books on other religions, desperately seeking the one that brought forth the most understanding and results. Little did I know that my already tainted spirit, would now become washed in the abyss of Satan's plan for me. God was not exalted in these moments. The further into doubt, confusion, and hopelessness that the enemy could bury me in, the further from God I would fall and eventually, face much detriment.

But I have a praying mother, that even though she had no idea what I was dealing with or going through she kept prayers over the heads of her children. At this time, which was the only shield of protection that I had, the prayers of my mother. I was too far gone to pray for myself.
I was broken, but I was not beyond repair. I had finally reached a point in my life, after many months, where I realized that there was no one greater than the greatest himself. This may have been my turning point, or at least one of many. After almost two years of being in a broken season,

I again, turned back to God. It came after the end of 2019, and the new year of 2020 was about to come in. I set a new year resolution to regain my life and to give it back to Christ. I was diligent about my new goal because the past year and a half had brought nothing but turmoil and dark days. I was stuck under the ocean, barely breathing, gasping for air, and only taking in more water. Unable to breathe for many days, it was a wonder that there was still even a pulse. Mentally I had checked out, but it was this proclamation of I am taking my life back from the enemy, which was about to catapult me into the greatest war that I had ever fought. A battle for myself, between me and Satan. A battle to get me back, because I was in his captivity for so long, and nothing good had come of it. Get thee behind me Satan, I belong to God! I would proclaim it, but I wasn't sure that I fully meant it, because remember, I was still trying to figure out who God even was. I knew of him, but did I know him for real? I didn't. But I wanted to.

I had confidence that I was about to enter the new year, as a new woman. I thought it was going to be easy. I had purchased inspirational books to indulge in, downloaded some of the best podcasts to keep my mind leveled, and was paying more attention to more motivational YouTube videos and in this time was introduced to the ministries of Sarah Jakes Roberts and Priscilla Shirer. I was beginning to feel like the broken pieces of me were starting to fixate themselves to be put back together again. I even began to change the kind of music I would listen to. I was so serious about the change this time. I was not going to be weak and allow my circumstances to cause me to dissociate myself from my God ever again. I had decided that I was going to be all in from this point on. I worked on regaining my prayer life. I still could not find the words to say aloud, so I began by writing. I would write my prayers on paper, because the words written seemed to make more sense to me than the words spoken. I had just released my first published book a couple months prior, how that book was even able to come to fruition is still a wonder to me. I was going to take this writing seriously, I assumed that possibly in the future, if I had written enough prayers, it could potentially become another book. I dwelled in the shadows of 2018 and 2019 broken. No one even knew, but my hope was to enter 2020, renewed. I wasn't going to be cold or lukewarm for God anymore. I was going to be all in, broken pieces and all.

December 29, 2019
10:17pm

Dear God,
Welcome back! I am genuinely welcoming you back into my life. You deserve to be here, and I deserve to live a life with you included in it.

Forgive me! I was unaware of the need to have you as the most intricate part of my daily living. I am sorry, very sorry. I know that the things that I have experienced these past few months have been solely because of my rejection towards you. I repent! I hope that you can forgive me once again as you have so many times before.

My life has been in shambles privately, whereas those on the outside looking in, feel I am at my greatest come up. I want to feel what they see. I want to be able to exude the happiness that others feel I showcase, and it be genuine and honest. I no longer desire to live a life in darkness, nor do I desire to live a life in false actions. God, I want you and I need you in my life. I have found that there is no one else that can help me out of my current state other than you. I constantly have placed blame on you for my recent circumstances, but I now recognize that all that has occurred has come from my own lack of accepting your guidance. My lack of following your voice and being obedient towards your direction. Forgive me. I was unable to accept what I did not understand.

I have been a troubled soul for such a long time, unable to reject the temptations from the enemy. You have shown me more than just a few times how forgiving you can be. I allowed the enemy to devour me, coming from many forms and in the people that I knew did not have my best interest at heart. I am tired! God, I am so tired!! Life has been exhausting and I can no longer live it without you. I am ready for my season to change. I am ready to see happier and brighter days. I am ready to live in the fullness of life, which I know that you desire for me.

I know that this will not happen overnight. I am fully aware that the first step is repentance, and I wholeheartedly do so! I can only pray that you accept.

You are a great God! Even when I blamed you and thought that you had left me for dead, to fend for myself, you always remained right there beside me, because of my lost soul, I was unable to feel your presence, but I ask that you open me up to know that you are always here with me. Open my heart and my soul to feel you once again! I want this to become my daily life and I desire to have you in it, I will be more consistent in my communication with you. My prayers will come in whatever form that I can bellow out, but they will come. For now, it is on paper. I pray that soon I will regain a posture of praise that the words that I write will be able to be announced in the form of highest praise to you! God, I need and want you here! I need you here for me, I need you here for Armani, Amaya, and Taylor! I need you here for my Mommy and my Daddy! I need you here for my brothers and my friends. Surround me with those whose hearts are equal to mine! Remove the enemies from my life who seek to devour me and remove me from your presence. I want a renewed heart and a renewed mindset. I want to walk closer with you than I ever have before. I want to know who you are personally, not by what I am told.

I want to feel you for myself. I want to experience your love in the most raw and genuine way. I want to walk with you daily and be guided by you, what you tell me to do, I will listen. When I fall, I want you to help me up. When I am confused, I want you to help me gain clarity. Where I am hurt, I want you to heal. I desire you and only you!

I want to be new! The old Desiree is no longer here, cultivate the new Desiree and mold me into what you would want me to be! I desire this!

God, I thank you for the things that you have done to keep me here! I thank you in advance for the things you will do to keep me here. I thank you for the faith and the belief that you hear me and will answer my prayers. I am all in!

Thank you for never leaving my side. Happy New Year! Happy New Me!

This and all other things, I ask in your son Jesus' name... AMEN!!!

I Blame God

GOOD GRIEF

The prayer that I wrote in my journal at the end of 2019, was probably more of a proclamation to war than it was a proclamation to the change that I desperately sought. Me, outwardly wanting to regain my relationship with God angered those from the darkness who wanted me to remain in the shadows along with them. The enemy had caught wind of my desire to stand tall again and be all in with my creator, and he was not going to make it an easy getaway. Had I known that I would soon face more troubles, more hurt, more agony, some far worse than the occurrences of my recent past, if I could have peeked into the future and realize what was to come, I probably would have told God, never mind, I changed my mind.

I thought that I was doing the right thing. I even found a new church home and joined the fellowship at the beginning of the new year in 2020 during the Covid-19 shutdown.
I was on track; I was fulfilling all the promises that I had told God that I would. I wanted to prove to him that I was a good child. My prayers that I continued to write in my journal became longer and longer as I began to express more of my desires and my thanks. It was within the first few weeks of the new year, and I truly felt that a change had come. Wow, that was easy!
Things were looking up and I was blessed. My mood was drastically brighter, and I had begun to cook more and spend more time with the kids. I would soon find that my natural

high would reach a very quick downward spiral back into the darkness and shadows where there was an easy grasp of the enemy's hands that I thought I had just escaped.

My father, who had been battling health issues and on dialysis for a few years very unexpectedly suffered a brain aneurysm and stroke at the end of February 2020. If anyone knew my father and knew me, then they were fully aware and knew that the relationship that we had, without question, was a unique and lovable father daughter connection. He was my best friend, father, biggest supporter, voice of reason and the only man that has ever spoiled me rotten. There was nothing that my father did not or would not do for me. Even when he would tell me no, amid my spoiled girl antics, he still made ways to keep me happy and smiling. My husband could not even compare to the level of princess treatment that I received from my dad; I think it kind of made him a little jealous that he fell short in that department. During the short tenure of our marriage, he would often ask, "Why do you have to call your dad for every little thing?" my response would always very arrogantly be "Because, he always fixes everything."

It was no secret that I was daddy's girl. Not everyone liked it either. We had the kind of relationship that could be envied. From a small girl I was on my dad's heels as much as he would allow. Once I became an adult, and had kids of my own, they then became his spoiled girls, still he never lacking from spoiling me. Random outings to the park, out for ice cream, shopping, or weekend trips to Myrtle Beach with my daughters were something that I think kept my dad feeling young. He was getting older, moving slower and with his kidney's failing and him being on dialysis three times a week, the girls kept him moving, and I always appreciated the breaks, especially during this time that I was now a single mother with three.

My dad had been in the hospital for a total of forty-eight hours before I had been made aware. It was on a Wednesday morning; my youngest daughter Taylor and I were heading to the outlet for some morning shopping and lunch. I was now a full-time entrepreneur working for myself. With my ex-husband not assisting with the cost for daycare, I could no longer work and afford my bills and daycare all by myself. I had decided that I would hustle my ass off to make ends meet, and that I did. This was also around the time that a very mysterious illness was beginning to plague the country they called Covid-19. No one knew what this virus was, but it was spreading fast! That morning, I received a text message from my half-brother telling me that dad was in the hospital. After receiving the quick details of where dad was, I turned my car around and headed to the hospital not far from my house. No less than twenty minutes after receiving the text from my brother, I got a call from my dad's only sister. This was strange to me because we did not often speak. I did not really have a close relationship with much of my dad's side of the family like my older brothers did, because I was usually with my mom's side of the family. I didn't even know that my aunt had my phone number. Upon the phone call and hearing her stammer and unable to find her words on the other end, I quickly gauged that my father's condition may have been more serious than let on by my brother via text. Still, I kept calm because I wanted to see him before I allowed my emotions and my thoughts to react.

When I entered the doors to the intensive care unit at the

hospital, I instantly was met with the trick of the enemy. This was undoubtedly going to be my first test in my proclamation to God that I wanted to be more like him. I know that I was not fully prepared for the chain of events that was to take place within the coming days and months, however, looking back, I know this was one of the seasons where God carried me instead of walking beside me. When we profess the things that we desire to have from God, he loves us enough to bless us with them, but only when he is confident that we are ready. How do you know if someone is ready for something? You test them. A student does not earn the degree before they are tested to have gained the knowledge. Knowledge in my prayer request is what I lacked at the time. I wasn't ready, in fact, I hadn't studied, nor had I had a well-balanced meal before testing time. I don't remember what my score was on the SAT's when I was in high school, I only remember the anxiety that I felt entering the testing room. Knowing that I was unprepared. I could hear my heart pounding above the proctor's instructions, and the sweat from my palms only made it more difficult to hold my pencil steady. This moment felt just like that day.

I continued down the hallway, which seemed to grow in length with every step that I took. The anxious feeling that I felt wanting to lay eyes on my father immediately retreated and became rage as I was approached and told that I could not enter. That anger was about to consume me, and cause me to become 2008 Desiree, the Desiree whose words cut like swords and chopped like an ax with no regard. The Desiree that many deemed crazy versus misunderstood and unheard. Instead, I took a deep breath, ignored the first barrier sent by the enemy and continued in peace to my destination. "Yes!" I thought to myself, I passed the first test! That was a weird thing to say, or even think, because that hurdle was nothing compared to what was on the way. Thinking back on those moments of tests, I am reminded of the story in the bible after Jesus fasted in the wilderness for forty days and forty nights.

When he had come out of his fasting, he was in a very vulnerable state, he was hungry, he was weak and filthy. Can you imagine not eating for forty days? I can't even go for four hours without at least a snack. So, just imagine how Jesus, the man, not Jesus the son of God, had felt. Soon as he came up out of the wilderness, there was the enemy ready and waiting to test him with his sickening self. Who really wants to take a test on an empty stomach? Satan tempted him with what he knew he may have wanted most within this moment, food! He advised him that if he is really who he says that he is, then turn the stones into bread so that he may eat.

Now, I don't know about you, but for those of you that know me, know how much of a point prover I like to be. Although I knew I didn't have to, I would have done it anyway just to prove to the enemy that I could, because who are you playing with?!
I guess that's why I'm not Jesus, and why Jesus is Jesus. I am chuckling because I can imagine me saying to the devil, "Boy move, let me show you! Cuz don't play with me!"
The whole purpose of Jesus's fast in the first place was so that he could draw closer to God, his father, and improve his prayer life. Sound familiar?

Just as I had stated in my written prayer at the end of 2019, Jesus to had sought to do the same!

The only difference was, I had not fasted. The proclamation alone was enough to send the tests and temptations. If the son of God had to endure tests, then who was I to not have to?

Ironically speaking, the number forty biblically signifies new life, new growth, transformation, and a change from one task to an even greater task. Are you all catching the revelation here? Jesus fasted for these forty days and these forty nights to emerge into the new life and growth that he sought in growing closer to God, and just as soon as he emerged, here comes the tests!

When I made claim to being all in, that was my emergence into a new life. It wasn't a forty day and night fasting, but those two years of turmoil, spiritual absence, sunken ships, regret, confusion, and more, I think were equal enough.

Once I had finally made my way into the ICU room where my father was, and my eyes had fallen on him, I am not sure exactly what I felt in that moment. I saw him lying there, still. There was no movement. There were tubes coming from his head, in his nose and all around him. Screens here and there reading one vital sign or another. Lord, another test so soon? I was beginning to reconsider my claim to being all in, but what in the world was happening? I was not prepared for this at all, where was the study guide?

I stood a few feet away from the hospital bed, just observing. I was looking for life, some sort of indication that he was alive. I didn't really have any emotion, I could not or did not want to cry. I wasn't sad, upset, or anything, I was just, still. Just there. I often think back to this moment, especially when the anniversary of my Father's death comes around. This was the first and the only time I had ever seen my father in such vulnerability, in a sense, he was in his own wilderness while he lay in that coma. I wonder was he seeking, or had he sought God? I remember asking the nurse that had come in to check his vitals if he could hear us. He replied that it would be hard to say, because some people while in a coma are able to hear and are aware of what is happening around them, while others are not.

I leaned further along in the hope that my father could hear, and that he knew and heard all that was transpiring around him. I grabbed his hand and asked, "What are you doing in here?"
I am not sure if I was expecting an answer from him, but in my mind, I heard his voice. I heard my father respond. I laughed out and said, "I hear you."
Blame it on my vast imagination that I have had since I was a child, but as I spoke to my father, he was answering me back and speaking to me within my mind. We were literally having a full-blown conversation while he said nothing. He was cracking jokes; I was chuckling and everything. If anyone else was in the room at that moment, they would've probably assumed that I was missing a few marbles. This moment was much like those that followed years later when I would speak with my other Father, my creator.

There was a conversation I was having with my mother on the phone one day, let me remind you, my mom is a minister and has been for over twenty years. She was raised in the traditional church under the A.M.E doctrine, we shall revisit this later. Anyways, in this conversation I was telling my mother how I felt so disconnected from God, and that I desired to hear him and speak with him. She advised me, that I needed to just talk to him, just like I was speaking on the phone with her, "Talk to him, he will hear you." is what she said. What did she mean? Just talk, like, open my mouth and just talk as though he is sitting right in front of me? That's weird, because ultimately, if God is a spirit and not a human, wouldn't I be talking to myself?

These, amongst other things, were the confusing parts about religion that I just could not seem to understand. Even when I tried to talk with God, as my mother suggested, I felt insane. I'm just sitting here talking to air, he isn't going to hear that. These doubtful moments made me question myself and my walk with God even more, because how could others so easily talk with God and know that he is listening, and I could not? I just didn't feel it, I didn't feel that he heard me, and even if he did hear me, how would I know what he was responding? Wouldn't I have to hear him talk back to me? But, at this moment sitting here with my father, I was doing the very thing that I previously stated before that I couldn't. That was God's way. I believe, of giving me that epiphany to inadvertently say to me, "...but I thought you said you couldn't do it? Look at you, doing it!"

After many days in the hospital, with no change in condition, my father passed away.

I was so angry. I was so hurt. I was so disappointed in God. Here I was, trying to change, trying to do better, praying more, I joined a church, I was doing everything I thought he wanted me to do, and he took the person away from me that I loved beyond anything in the entire world. He took my father! Now God, is this another test? Because I can tell you now, I will not ace this one!

With all the events surrounding my father's death up to the day he was buried, I know was sent to send me into a rage, but I remained quiet. I don't even think my silence was intentional, I just believe that I was in such a state of shock that I couldn't react to anything or anyone. I had experienced deaths in my family before, my grandmother, my Uncle John, my cousin's Patrick and Chris, a former romantic interest that died in car accident, all people that I loved and cared about, but there was something different about the death of my father. This was my parent, one of my pro-creators of life. This death made me numb. I probably could have gotten hit by a bus and not even say ouch. I was angry... with God. The little bit of religion that I was trying to gain, I felt slipping away. Not only did God take my father, but he also took away my desire to seek him more, because I had to deal with grief, in whatever form that was to soon come.

What made this transition even worse was the fact that the entire country went on shutdown the week following my father's funeral due to the Covid-19 pandemic. No one could go to restaurants, stores, or do anything. No one could even go to work unless they were an essential worker. People were dying left and right; hospitals were full, and people were afraid because no one really knew what was happening. GOOD GRIEF CHARLIE BROWN! But I was saying good grief God! You are to blame for all of this! I BLAME GOD!

I Blame God

ISOLATION

The Covid-19 Pandemic had taken the world by surprise. No one really knew what it was, the cause or the cure. Although this virus was rattling the world, my focus was on something much different, and that was maneuvering grief. This was new for me, something I had not yet experienced to this capacity and yet I had to do so during a worldwide lockdown. The desperation of not wanting to feel grief was a goal for me. I didn't want to sit in my room and cry every day, I didn't want to shed tears every time I looked at my father's pictures, or every time someone called to ask how I was doing. I would do things daily to avoid having to sit with myself and deal with it. That thing was mostly alcohol, overeating and lashing out on my social media posts about how awful a person my father's companion was and blaming his death on her as well. I was not in a good space mentally, physically, and certainly not spiritually.

Why would God wait until the moment that I assumed that I was getting my life together to want to hit me with this? God hated me. He didn't want me to succeed in life, he wanted me to constantly be at his mercy all the time, and I was not about that life. I wanted him to give me the good stuff, like he was doing for everyone else. Let me be wealthy. Give me the luxury vehicle. I want a nice house. Where is my perfect husband? Do you have nothing good for me God?

Those were my thoughts. Blessings were skipping over me and landing on the heads of others, others that I didn't think

were all that deserving. Let me pause here and take us back to a few scriptures, because, well, remember, that is where the promises of God reside. Let's visit **Matthew 5:4** "Blessed are they that mourn, for they shall be comforted." and **Psalm 34:18** "The Lord is near to the brokenhearted and saves the crushed in spirit." and boy was my spirit crushed! More like stepped on, stomped on, rolled over by a semi-truck and thrown over a cliff. What made it even more crushing was that I was not prepared. Had I had more time to plan, more time to think, more time to gather my thoughts, more time to just get ready for what was to come, I feel I would have been better off. But again, let's revert to the promises and instructions laid out for us in scripture, **Matthew 24:42-44** "Therefore keep watch, because you do not know the day nor the hour the Lord will come. Understand this; if the master of the house had known the hour the thief should come he would keep watch and not allow his house to be broken into. So, you also must be ready, because the son of man will come at a time when you do not expect him."
Although this scripture talks about the return of Jesus, I feel it can also be used in this situation, as had I been prepared, the blow would not have hit as hard, the sting would not hurt so bad, and the consuming thoughts would be more logical versus emotional. I should have prepared. But how? How do you prepare for something such as this? The answer is, through prayer!

When in prayer it is up to us to ask for the right things. Yes, we can ask for the big house, the nice car, the high paying job, and the perfect mate, but we can't forget to ask for the things that are far less tangible as well. We must ask for peace of mind, understanding, wisdom, the ability to remain

strong in adversity, willpower, and tenacity to continue through obstacles. What I failed to do then was ask for these things, and how could I when I didn't even know that I was supposed to? The saying goes, that when you know better, you do better. Had I been more mature in my spiritual journey then, I would have recognized the need for more prayer during my time of grief and isolation, versus blame and anger. It was the blame and anger that made the grief process much more difficult. Think of the death of my father as a stab wound, or a very deep cut. I bandaged it up, but I didn't stitch it up. It still bled, a lot. It was still an open wound, and I failed to ask in prayer for God to heal the open wound. So, the enemy, recognizing my vulnerable state of mind, began to drop foreign objects down into my open wound. Anger, blame, sadness, and adding insult to injury, something that I had no control over, isolation. As these things were deposited into my open wound, an infection grew. Guess what the infection was, did you guess spiritual disconnect?
BINGO!! Again, I became disconnected from God, and all that I wanted from him.

My lack of understanding at that time, gave me a falsified outlook on who I thought God was, or who I thought he should be. He didn't love me, if he did, I wouldn't be feeling like this. Again, I blamed God for my current life circumstance because it was his fault. We have all been alive long enough to know that no one lives forever, I don't care how good or bad a person may be, just as sure as you are born, you must die. Because death is such an inevitable occurrence, why do we not prepare ourselves more for it? Now, do not misconstrue my notion here, death will hurt! Especially a close death, like a parent, spouse, or child, you are going to feel that, and you will be immersed in grief, and that is okay. What is not okay is dwelling there and placing blame. Who would really be to blame? God?

During this isolation period, I fell deeper into a black hole, and again, no one knew. I immersed myself in my businesses, because making and spending money made me feel better, another unhealthy habit that we will revisit later in this book. Because there were very few options to do much of anything, this was the time that I should had taken to just be with God and God alone, I had nothing but time and opportunity, however, I fumbled the ball. Instead, I found fault in everything that happened while I was in this space. I can imagine God sitting next to me during these moments, just watching me with face in palm as I continued to train my thoughts to be more pessimistic than optimistic and make the wrong decisions concerning his plan for me. This was yet another test that I was not doing so well on. I will admit, I have never been a good test taker. In school, I would ace the class work and understand the assignments but fail the tests miserably. It was no different for me in real life. Had my spiritual maturity been a thing, I would have been able to see the good in this isolation. Want me to prove to you how isolation can be a good thing? Well, let's head over to, yes, correct, that book of promises and instructions. The scriptures.

Do not confuse this example of isolation as being lonely or isolated in a negative way. Scripture does warn against isolation as losing sense of sound judgement and being unwise, however, in this instance, isolation was beyond my control and considering where I was trying to be in my spiritual walk, I should have used this time as a season to

draw closer to him, not further away. We must find solitude in order to hear from God and remove ourselves from the noise of the world and our everyday routines so that we can prioritize our time with him.
Psalm 91 "He that dwelleth in the secret place of the most high shall abide under the shadow of the almighty."

What is the secret place? The secret place can be your car, your bedroom, a closet, it is simply your most intimate moment and space with the creator. A place of refuge, peace, safety, and rest. The secret place is where we commune with God, in this place, we should find that there is nothing or no one more important to us than God. This moment is our time to be alone with him and speak to him, supp with him, pray to him. When in this secret place, we abide under his shadow, meaning he covers us in this moment. Here, we are restored, refreshed, we are protected, and he rejoices when we enter this place with him. Why am I telling you all of this?
I am telling you because these are the things that I wish that I knew, or that I wish someone had told me so that my spiritual journey or learning to maneuver it, wouldn't have been so top heavy.

Maneuvering life trying to do the right things, but also not losing yourself as the unique person that you are can be tricky at times. Anyone that knows me personally knows that I have lived my life solely by being very transparent, fun, funny and just living life on my own terms. Always wanted to be known for keeping it real, no faking or pumping to ever make people believe that I was something or someone that I was not. I know too many of those types of people and I look at them sideways every time, because who are you trying to fool? Yourself? Because I am not convinced. I never wanted that to be me, but in living life in that way, it came as a detriment to my relationship with my creator. I have learned over the years that I can still be me; I can be transparent, honest, and real and still please God. Learning to maneuver this version of myself has been tricky, but I share with you in hopes that you gain your own sense of your personal spiritual journey, you may learn something from me, and you may not, but my satisfaction comes from just sharing my story with you, it's my testimony.

Though I needed this isolation to be something that enhanced my mood and my journey, it did the complete opposite. I had entered a land of wilderness, unable to find the road that would lead me out. The wilderness was scary, I saw myself in a light that I did not recognize. I was afraid. Still, as terrified as I was, God was still working on me. While in the wilderness, he allowed me the time and space that I needed to see myself and my heart as it was in its current state. This was the place of spiritual chastisement that I reached. This was another step in the process that I needed to experience. He led me here; it was another test. Because I declared that I wanted to be all in with him, he had to test me to make sure that I wasn't just pulling his leg. Guess where I found the confirmation for that revelation? Did you say the scripture? No? Well, that is where I found it. If you haven't realized it by now, scripture will be used a lot, because I want to show you how regardless of how we feel or what we deal with in life there is some sort of instruction or confirmation in the word to help us through. You don't have to be a bible scholar, because I most certainly am not, however, when I have had questions, this is where he leads me every time for an answer.

Deuteronomy 8:2 "And thou shalt remember all the way which the Lord thy God led thee these forty years in the wilderness, to humble thee and to prove thee, to know what was in thine heart, whether thou would keep his commandments or not."
Do you recognize that number forty again? Even in our darkest and most undeveloped place, he still resides. The wilderness, by definition, is nothing more than an undeveloped land where there are no habitations. The dessert. Isolated land. Are you catching this like I am giving it?
 In my underdeveloped mind, the proclamation of wanting to reside and dwell within him more was enough to be cast into spiritual wilderness, so that he could test me and assure that I meant what I said. What I saw and experienced in the physical, was just God's way of taking me through the wilderness in the spiritual. When I thought he had left me in the middle of nowhere, he was right there with me, watching and waiting to see what my next move would be. The isolation wasn't a curse. Yet, I blamed God.

# I Blame God

SAY THAT SAME PRAYER

My grandmother, whom we called Mag, was a woman of much strength and one who very clearly knew God. She had endured so much, yet still gave all her praises to God. Her dedication to being a servant to him and sowing into good ground was evident in her life living. My grandmother had nine children, four of her nine are preachers, my mother included. You would assume that God had great favor over my grandmother to have blessed her with four children that are dedicated to the teaching of the gospel. The upbringing that she provided for her nine children as a widow woman, clearly included God as the head of their lives. She knew where her help came from. Imagine raising nine children alone. That by itself is enough to continuously have one calling on the Lord.

As a child, I did not recognize my grandmother as the woman of God that I later saw her as. She was simply just my grandmother. The woman who's house I took the bus to after school. The woman that always had a hot meal for her children and grandchildren with the sweetest jug of Kool-Aid you ever had. The woman that killed chickens in the backyard with her bare hands and cleaned hog heads in the kitchen sink. The community kitchen hairstylist and nurse. Mag was a staple in the Pineland community where she lived. In church, she served on the choir and as the church housekeeper. She was all these things, but most importantly, she was wise. Her gift from God was wisdom, and she instilled that same wisdom into her children and her grandchildren. Her wisdom was sometimes very comical, she loved to laugh. I can remember as kids, my cousins and I would be riding our bikes back and forth on the dirt road alongside Mag's house, or playing in the woods or blackberry bushes nearby and we could hear my grandmother's cackles and laughter from whatever distance we were from her porch conversations with her visiting friends. Everything about my grandmother embodied strength, elegance, poise, wisdom, and a heart for God. I wish that I could sit and have conversations with her now about my own journey. I am sure she would have wise words of encouragement, much like the things she said to her four preaching children while they maneuvered their spiritual journeys.

Mag had a way with words. Her many sayings, often misunderstood, later in life became guides as to how to handle everyday life occurrences. Like, the one she often stated to my cousin's and I if we were too rambunctious when she was watching her soap operas or the evening news, "hunna know wha papa say bout the happy bird init?" and we would all know then to settle down, she wouldn't even have to finish the rest of the saying. We would all sit and be still, while all of our eyes fixated on her. We knew what Papa said about the happy bird, but we would dare not finish the phrase. Once she had our attention, she would complete and say, "e shit up the nest." Understand, I grew up in rural South Carolina, so the dialect was not spoken using proper verbiage. In charismatic Mag fashion, it was her most subtle way of telling us to calm down and be quiet. The messing up of the nest was going to be us getting chopped with whatever she could find in her reach if we failed to comply. The reference of the happy bird became something I would use in my adult life, because anytime I found myself becoming too excited about a thing, whether it be a business idea, romantic interest, job transition or anything, I would try not to get too excited and anxious so as to not ruin the opportunity, or the nest.

My grandmother's spirituality shined bright in her daily tasks. Washing the dishes, cooking dinner, sweeping, mopping, and folding laundry, her thing was to always sing old hymns while she completed her tasks. I used to love hearing her sing around the house, sometimes I would join in song with her, to me, I was just singing a song with my grandmother, however, what I didn't understand then was how the singing of those hymns brought much comfort to her soul during times of either turmoil or reflection. A moment to reflect on how far God had brought her would cause the bellowing of a hymn or a simple "Thank you Lord." or the receiving of a bill that she knew she was unable to pay, prompted a "I know the Lord will make a way, oh yes he will." in song. She was so in tuned with God, and with the holy spirit that she recognized a proclamation through song and words would bring success or completion to whatever the thing was. You know what else that is called? Faith. **Hebrew 11:1** "Now faith is the substance of things hoped for, the evidence of things not seen."

Imagine, trusting and believing in God so much, having such a spiritual connection that you believe the Father would fix a thing if all you did was believe that he would. What a gift. Faith that never wavers. I deeply desired this for myself. I passionately wanted God to love me so much that he would grant me with the gifts that he had given my grandmother. Faith and wisdom. There had been so many times that I wanted God to fix a thing, but because I didn't believe he fully cared about me, I didn't believe he would grant me these desires or that I was even deserving of him doing so. I had been a wretch undone, and in my disconnect, chose to find my own ways in bringing forth completeness to my own issues. Why ask God, after all, he was to blame for these circumstances. He allowed them to happen, so why would he fix them? I was not worthy of the things I had been asking of him. I didn't even go to church service regularly. I didn't tithe, I cussed, a lot! I drank and got drunk in the clubs, I was having sex and I liked it. Who was I to be so deserving of such a gift as Faith?

As I grew into adulthood, the many sayings Mag bestowed became affirmations.
Even in her absence, her children and grandchildren could often reference back to her wise aphorisms and be comforted to keep going. The one I believe that we all reference the most, "Say that same prayer.", my grandmother, through faith, believed that if we continued to ask God for a thing, no matter how long we had to ask, that eventually it would be granted. My mother, aunts and uncles often sit in discussion at our family gatherings, offering their testimonies as to how "saying that same prayer" eventually brought forth success to their circumstance. I have even been able to contribute accolades to Mag's legacy by stating my own a time or two as well. Mag was so spiritually connected that she knew that asking in prayer would grant results.
Mark 11:24 tells us plainly "therefore I tell you, whatever you ask in prayer, believe that you have received it, and it will be yours.," not only should we ask for what it is we need in prayer, but we should also ask with good motives. Want that confirmed in scripture?

James 4:3 "when you ask, you do not receive because you ask with wrong motives, that you may spend what you receive on your pleasures."
He wants us to ask him for things, and another thing that Mag taught us, was that when you ask in prayer, the stamp that mails it to heaven or review and fulfillment, is to ask it in Jesus's name.
John 14:13 "and I will do whatever you ask in my name, so that the Father may be glorified in the Son. You may ask me for anything in my name, and I will do it."

Mag was on to something here. The clearest evidence that I can vividly recall of receiving something that I had to "say that same prayer" concerning, has been the relationship that my oldest daughters have with their father. Man, did I pray! When my first husband and I divorced, it was messy from the beginning to the very end. Not only did we have domestic issues, but support for the kids had to be sorted out and both of us had already moved on romantically with new partners before the judge could even sign the decree. We were young and reckless with our love and with the loss of our marriage, unfortunately, the girls suffered as a result. I felt that because I was partly responsible for this situation, I had to overcompensate in the areas where their father lacked. He and I had very little dealings, because of it, he had very little dealings with the girls as well. Within a three-year timespan after the finalization of our divorce, I can count on one hand how many weekends the girls spent with him. This, to me, was not a normal occurrence, as my father was always involved and a very intricate part of my life even after his divorce from my mother. I always assumed it normal that both parents be heavily involved in their kids' lives, as this was what I observed.

It came as a burden to me to grapple with the fact that this was the total opposite for my daughters. My overcompensation soon wore me out, as I inadvertently filled both roles. Causing more stress on our daily lives that I could realize at the time. I thought I was doing the right thing. Giving my girls what I assumed they needed. They didn't need a mother trying to be a father, they needed their mother to be their mother, only their father could be their father. Others on the outside looking in, deemed me supermom, having no idea of the disservice that I was committing. Being the overcompensate mother was not a badge of honor. I soon found myself pleading for a break. I needed to be something other than a mom 24/7. I wanted to have a social life, hang out with my friends, and go out on dates. I was beginning to resent being a single mother, and those frustrations came out in my language and actions towards my children. I was forcing them to own the delusion that they were the reason our lives were more difficult than the average. I not only blamed God, but I also blamed my children.

I realized that this was unhealthy. This was not the way that a good mother should conduct, I was promoting trauma in my home, and I was saddened by the revelation. Everything about this needed to change, and it was up to me to do so. The outcome would ultimately begin with how I chose to handle it. Thanks to my grandmother and her wisdom, I decided to handle it with prayer. I focused solely from that point forward on being a great mother, because that was all that I had the capacity to be. I said that same prayer for my children, their father, and their relationship, in hopes that God would turn the situation around. After years of prayers, with no change in circumstance, I questioned God immensely. Sir, have you heard this prayer? What number am I in queue? Do you have a voicemail where I can leave a message? I was becoming weary with the same routine and not seeing any results. My kids needed a father. In desperation, I accepted the acquaintance of someone whom I thought God had sent to be a father figure. Maybe his intent was to not change their own father, but to send someone who would be like a father to them. My prayers had finally been answered after years of saying that same prayer. It finally happened. Imagine how happy I was to see the fruits of faith through prayer. However, I couldn't be more wrong.

I focused so heavily on what I wanted out of this ordeal that I never asked my children what they wanted or how they felt. I was happy, and they were miserable. They didn't tell me until months after my separation from the one whom I thought to be a father figure to them, that they never liked him. They expressed to me all of the things over the years that they were disgruntled about concerning this makeshift father, daughter relationship. I thought they adored him, and cared about him as much as I had, but not only was my connection to God lost during this time, but my connection to my kids was gone too. Had I had more discernment, I would have been able to recognize why this situation was not a good one. Here is where I am going to kick you in the gut, even when we pray to our father which arts in heaven, the enemy hears those same prayers. Satan listens and schemes a plan to give you exactly what it is that you are praying for, but with malicious intent. Confusing right? I know because I was too. When you understand the tricks of the enemy, then you will know how to resist his temptations. First and foremost, Satan has no power and no authority. He cannot do anything without being given direction by God, but when he is made aware of your desires, he can, and he will trick you into believing that you are receiving a thing as a blessing. That is why discernment is so important. How do you gain discernment? By wisdom and understanding. How do you gain wisdom and understanding? By reading and studying the word AND by asking for it in prayer. Say that same prayer.

1 Kings 3:9 "Give therefore thy servant an understanding heart to judge thy people, that I may discern between good and bad; for who is able to judge this thy so great a people? This scripture is when Solomon asked God for discernment, wisdom and understanding. God was pleased with him for doing so and granted him what he had asked.

Anyway, back to the point at hand. My discernment lacked, therefore, I only recognized what the enemy sent as a distraction versus a blessing from God. Do not take this the wrong way, I am not saying that the person himself was a bad person, it was the strong desire and my lack of knowledge and understanding that made that situation bad. Upon this forfeiture of what I had hoped to be a father for my daughters, turned me back to having to yet again say that same prayer. God was sick of me, honestly, I was sick of him at this point too. Yet again, he had led me to a frustrating time in my life that I assumed was over. This journey was not going as easily as I had hoped, I was ready to give it up. Just forget all of it, my children and I would be fine. We didn't need the father, nor did we need God. Life was still fine without either. That's what I made myself believe. My upbringing and tugs from my grandmother from the afterlife, however, caused me to continue to pray for a change. I don't even think I truly believed that there ever would be any difference, I just did it because, well, I was kind of led to.

Thirteen years later, after continuously proclaiming that same prayer, a change had come, and you already know who is to blame for this sudden change of circumstances, I blame God!

I Blame God

PUT A PRAISE ON IT!

Growing up as a preacher's kid, and in a very religious household, I bore witness to a lot of things that took place within the church. Some of it frightened life right out of me on most occasions, but a lot of it traditionally became a way of life, things that I just knew to do or not to do when I entered the house of the Lord. For example, whenever the ushers of the church stood at the doors, which meant this was not a time to go in or out of the sanctuary. So even if you felt as though you were about to hurl right in the middle of service, you had better swallow it until the ushers directed you to be able to step outside or to the restroom. On first Sunday's, we partook in the Lord's Supper, or communion. During that time, you were not to speak, not to move, you could barely blink, as this was deemed one of the most sacred times of service. I grew up under the doctrine of the African Methodist Episcopal Church, founded by Bishop Richard Allen in 1816. This is going to matter later in this chapter, and you will see why.

Everything about the church that I grew up in was very meticulous.
There was a rule and a strategy or organization to everything, there was very little room for free will or free range within the AME church. Even to become a minister within the AME church, there was a process. You could not, and you were not going to wake up one morning and announce that you had been called to preach, well, you could, but it would not be received well. There was a process and educational classes to endure before you could even become licensed for

the assignment. This may be where my OCD for being very organized began. If you know anything about being a part of the YPD also, then, well, I can almost bet that you have a career in some field that requires much organization and attention to detail. Like, my career is in Human Resources, so my foundation in the church from whence I came may have a small 3% part to play in that. I was elected the delegate for every YPD conference, having to take notes and record minutes at all the meetings at the tender age of eleven, even having to speak in front of hundreds of my peers, so yes, the members of the YPD learned very early on about public speaking, note taking and such.

Another tradition that probably began my road of conviction was the tradition of receiving the holy ghost. We had been taught that our parents carried the weight of our sins until we reached the age of accountability, which was deemed to be the age of twelve. Twelve being the significant number because Jesus was twelve when he began to demonstrate his understanding of right from wrong when he ditched his parents to go speak with the elders in the temple during Passover. If you are unfamiliar with that story, read about it in the book of Luke.
Every year, my church held a week long revival right before Easter Sunday. Any child in the church that was twelve, or nearing the age of twelve, was to be at this revival and made to tarry at the altar each night of service, in hopes of receiving the gift of the holy spirit. One of those five nights, you'd better believe there was some child shouting, crying, and confessing to God that they now take the accountability from their parents to themselves. To those that received the gift, there would be a baptism they took part in during sunrise service on Easter Sunday morning, to symbolize

their walk with God from thence forward. The child would be given their own bible, as a gift from the church, and a certificate that also went on record within the church to say that you had now received the gift of the holy spirit and been baptized.

If you have ever been to a tarrying service as a kid, it was probably the most traumatizing thing to have ever been forced to experience. Imagine just wanting to be at home with your dolls, snacks and watching TGIF on a Friday night, but instead you are in a church with adults shouting and passing out all around you, loud music from organs, drums and tambourines pouring into your ears, and kneeling at the altar with a mother of the church or a deacon yelling in your ear to say "Jesus, Jesus, Jesus, Jesus!" until you felt something shift within your body, that would then cause you to jump around the church and shout yourself, or purge into a nearby trash can with an usher assisting you. TRAUMATIZING!
Nonetheless, it was the tradition, or the right of passage to receive this wonderful gift from God. If you were one of the lucky ones to experience the holy ghost, then you were special. You were important and favored by God. If you didn't, well, you were brought back the next year to try again. Now, whether this group of my twelve-year-old peers had been feeling something, or truly caught the holy spirit, I cannot attest to, however, at twelve years old, I was not thinking about being gifted with the holy ghost. Do you really want me, at twelve, to allow a ghost to enter my body, take control of me to the point to where I was flailing all over the sanctuary, crying and out of breath just to say I believe in God? My mind was more on getting home before Family Matters went off so that I could see if Laura finally decided

to give Steve Urkel a kiss or a date. The mind of a child that young I felt was not yet mature enough to understand the weight of what was being put on us. Now that we had to symbolically carry and be responsible for our own sins, you mean to tell me that when I would sail a cussword on the playground, which would be a mark against me and not my mother or father. My parents would probably tear me a new butthole if they had been made aware of all the sins I committed before the age of twelve that they had to take responsibility for. Furthermore, have you ever met my six-year-old Taylor?
That child innocently steals and lies more than enough, am I currently taking on her sins? Lord, I surely hope not.

By the time I became an adult, I do not think that I can truly say I had ever felt the holy ghost. What did it even feel like exactly? There had been times where I had been emotionally moved by a song, a sermon or a moment during worship service where I have shed tears and been made to fall into the arms of the person standing next to me, or the prophet prophesying to me, but was that the holy ghost, or just a vulnerable moment? Later in life, I joined a Holiness Pentecostal church, and let's just say, growing up as an AME, that transition was one to surely document. If you know, then you know. This church, from its order of service to the ordaining of his Pastors, Bishops, and Elders, was much different from what I had been accustomed to. Even the shouting that took place was different. In the AME church that I grew up in, yes, I witnessed people catching the holy spirit, but if you went too long in your praise, the pastor was surely to mount the pulpit and that would be your que to calm it down and have a seat. In the holiness church, you had free range to shout for as long as you felt the spirit, even if it was for two hours. No one sat you down, in fact, you would be encouraged to continue by the musicians who would continuously change the tempo on a click track, the wailing of the church mothers seated on the front row, and other church goers from the audience who would hop up, grab you by the arm and help you shout because in the house of holiness, nobody shouts alone.

I would watch these theatrics, and honestly, I enjoyed it. It had become the most entertaining part of my Sunday, and I would have been a little disappointed when I did attend church and the spirit wasn't high enough to cause the show to begin. After many, many years of attending church myself, and being somewhat moved by the message or the songs and music, I wondered, why had I never received this special gift? What was wrong with me? Was my holy ghost button broken, or was I not special enough to my God to be gifted with receiving the holy spirit? How come all these people around me could do the Jesus bop, not to be confused with the Diddy bop, and I could not? Was I even doing church the right way?

This revelation often made me feel a kind of way, I don't know if it was sadness, but more so, embarrassment if anything. When the preacher would often state, "Turn to your neighbor and shout, YES LORD.," I never wanted to turn to my neighbor, because why are we yelling at each other in church? I think my neighbor heard you just as well as I did. Why do I have to repeat what you are already saying? These are the exact thoughts that I would have during sermons from the preachers that did this type of thing, but why? I wanted to be a better worshipper, I wanted to shout, I wanted to yell at my neighbor and do all the things a good church goer and lover of God did. I often felt that my relationship with God must had been so tarnished and withdrawn that I could never and would never be anything more than the girl that would just sit on the pew looking lost.

I just could not figure out how to do church right.
I didn't shout, purge or run around the sanctuary. Because of this, I never felt that God had felt me worthy enough to gift me with the holy spirit. Did God not like me? Was I not worthy? Surely, I had to had been more worthy than the man shouting up and down the aisles who was cheating on his wife, or the woman that was voluntarily sleeping with the lady's husband that lived a few doors down from her. Was I not more worthy than that young woman with the four kids and four different baby fathers? She was shouting with her wide butt having to be covered up by the ushers and a white sheet, were these people more worthy than I?
My confusion was what the holy spirit was versus what I was seeing with my own eyes being done in the church Sunday after Sunday.

Let's dissect. This understanding took many years, and certainly lots of reading and clarity. I had to basically forget all that I knew, or thought that I knew, and all that I had been taught. That is the first step in seeking God for yourself, forget everything you know and have been taught and forget the traditions that you were raised upon, most of those traditional things that we know and practice, will cause you to remain lost and unable to know who God really is to you, it is a personal thing. First, the holy spirit is not what we see in the flesh of those theatrics parading up and down the aisles and in the sanctuary during church service. The Holy Spirit is wisdom, understanding, fear of the Lord, accepting guidance from the Lord, obeying him, walking by the spirit, exercising your faith, being convicted when you sin, the enabling to pray and understand God's word, temperance, the Holy Spirit helps you to recognize and understand the truth in your search and walk with God. That is what the Holy Spirit is! If you have these things, then you have the gift!

The shouting that we bear witness to is the praise! **Psalm 47:1** says, "Clap your hands, all people. Shout to God with loud songs of joy." Shouting is a form of worship that can be made in celebration, supplication or intercessory. Basically, the shout that we see people carry on with is the thank you for something God has done, that is why sometimes in church, the preacher will say, "If God has ever done anything for you, I dare you to shout and give him glory right now." You would then see half the congregation go into a fit of praise, which is saying "Thank You" to God for what he had done. Or, the preacher may say, "If you are believing God to fix something for you, shout a praise to him for this thing to happen." And again, half the congregation would shout in praise, to put a praise on what God is about to do, or what they are believing he will do, a praise of faith!

Psalm 149:3 says, "Let them praise his name with dancing, praise him with tambourine and dance." And let's not forget the most famous shouting man of them all, David.

2nd Samuel 6:14 "and David danced before the Lord with all of his might, and David was girded with a linen ephod."

What we see is the praise of having the Holy spirit. Praises of thanksgiving. Praises of fix it for me Lord. Faith praises. Praises of Love for the Father. Praises of, look how far you brought me. Praise is the stamp on receiving the gift. I had the gift and didn't even know it. I received the gift when I first confessed that I wanted Christ to enter my life, and that

I wanted a personal relationship with him. The gift was received when I became stronger in him, wiser in him, when I allowed myself to become vulnerable for him, and seek the truth, I received the gift of the Holy Spirit. The shouting was another form of worship. There are many different types and ways to worship, Yadah (worship by lifting hands), Tehillah (to sing), Barak (to kneel), Halal (to praise boastfully/clamorously), Towdah (worship in adoration), Zamar (worship with instruments), Shabach (worship/praise with a loud tone or shout).

So, my Holy Ghost button was never broken, nothing was wrong with me because I did not feel an urge to jump around or climb the walls of the sanctuary. There was nothing to be embarrassed about because I didn't dance like David danced, my praise was just different. I didn't have to do what everyone else did, because again, this was personal, and personally, I like the way I shout, praise and worship. It took the personal search of what God means to me and how I see him and how he sees me. I won't know him as you know him, you won't know him as I know him, and we won't know him as our neighbors, our parents, our children, our spouses, or our best friends know him. We will only know him as we know him for ourselves. **Proverbs 8:17** "I love those who love me, and those who seek me diligently find me."

I went looking for him, I found him, and I am building the most intimate relationship with him, because this was what my heart desired. I wouldn't have known better if I didn't seek better, and for that, I blame God.

CONTROL THE TRAUMA

Do you know what trauma is? We have all experienced trauma in one way or another at some point in our lives. Whether it be a physical injury, or an experience that changed how you view a thing, a person, a place, or a situation, trauma has happened to all of us. We may not have recognized it as such, or even called it that, but for me, trauma was a norm that I had always been able to easily pinpoint and say, this is traumatic. The hurt, the scars, the wounds, the cuts both physically and emotionally were things that I would tend to just deal with. Of all the trauma I have endured throughout life, the most traumatic thing for me, and you probably would have never guessed this, has been being a mother.

A thing that my daughters and I always joke about is the fact that I was always very vocal about never having wanted kids yet ended up with three. In my high school Senior year memory book, there was a page where you describe what your future will be like after high school. My seventeen-year-old self boldly stated that I didn't want any children, I wanted to marry a military man and just travel the world with my husband. Who knew that I would end my Senior year as a mother and then a wife three months later. Not what I had planned, but, if you want to make God laugh, tell him the plans you have for yourself right?

If you have ever met either of my three children, you would know that they are all very different, yet very much the same. They all enjoy being around me, literally, like shadows. If we are in a public setting, you will find them all within less than two feet away from me, standing or sitting very close by like little ducklings following their mother around. My oldest, however, in our more private settings, can always be found in her bedroom with the door closed, she will be on the phone with her little boyfriend, she's seventeen soon to be eighteen by the time this book is released, or in the mirror doing her hair or even finding her latest fashion haul on SHIEN or Fashion Nova. You can find my middle daughter, the sixteen-year-old, in my room, lying across my bed filling me in on all the latest high school drama, and letting me know that her school is very ghetto. If I am in the kitchen cooking, or in the living room watching tv, you'd find her there too. Wherever I am, there she will be also, just like Jesus, ha ha ha! Then, there is my youngest, the baby of the bunch and the spoiled one that thinks she can get away with anything. She demands attention wherever she is, and makes it known that she does not care about rules. She will do whatever she must to make sure that someone sees her, even if that means climbing on my computer desk and jumping from it, touching her sisters' belongings, eating, or drinking in the bedroom, which she knows is a huge no in my house. She tests the limits with no regard to the consequences.

Regardless of their differences or similarities, my love for them is and has always been the same and has been consistent over the years of their existence. Though my desire was never to become a mother, much less a single mother, I have found reward in having little Desiree's to fill the world with more greatness, more love, more smiles, and more attitude. What has primarily been the most rewarding and the most victorious part of my entire life, has also been the most traumatic. I know that some of you are probably clutching your pearls, because when you see me, you see a great mother. You see someone who loves her children and who has raised them and is raising them to be model citizens. All true indeed, however, to understand why motherhood has been so traumatic for me, you must first understand trauma. It has taken me months and months of therapy to understand myself and why motherhood has been such a triggering experience for me. First, let's make sure that we have a good grasp on what trauma really is.

Trauma can be emotional, it can be physical too, but in this sense, we are going to talk about the emotional trauma. Trauma is the emotional response to a terrible event, such as an accident, a rape, or a death. Immediately after said event, the shock of the event typically will bring forth unpredictable emotions, flashbacks, strained relationships, and even physical symptoms like headaches, nausea, and added stress on your joints. Acute trauma stems from one traumatic event, like a bad car accident. Chronic trauma is caused by prolonged events such as domestic abuse and complex trauma is caused by varied and multiple traumatic events of an invasive or interpersonal nature. If I had to guess the type of trauma that I inconveniently have been forced to manage, I would say it is the latter, complex trauma.

Now, do not misinterpret my reasoning here. Becoming a mother has not been traumatic. The actual conception of my babies did not guarantee anything more than a good time. The forty weeks, sometimes less, of pregnancy wobbling around like a duck, and giving birth did not garnish what I have deemed as trauma. Well, unless we are discussing my middle daughter's birth, which was done without an epidural, all natural, and in no way shape or form with a birthing plan in mind, then yes, I guess we could say that was a tad bit traumatic. The events that have taken place being a mother are what has caused this complex trauma and PTSD. One event that I think has caused the majority of this was the medical diagnosis of my middle daughter. Had I known that all three of my children would have some sort of medical condition, I probably would have knocked on God's front door myself and in my most comical, but dark humor nature, yelled through the peep hole "Hey Bruh! Come outside. We need to talk.," as I am rolling back my sleeves and putting up my fists ready to engage in confrontation which would surely end in a brawl of some sort. I was not prepared to be a mother, I wasn't prepared to be a single mother, and I surely was not prepared to be a single mother to three disabled children. Luckily, or should I say, Blessingly, the conditions that my children have has not limited their way of life, it has just adhered to more caution. My oldest, an asthmatic and having limited vision in her left eye, still drives, is on the color guard team at her school, and does all the things a typical bougie teenager does. My youngest, with her sickle cell diagnosis, though this can be a very debilitating disease, we have been blessed that she has not had a crisis since she was three years old, almost five years ago. Let's all pause and knock on a piece of wood here.

It was the diagnosis of my middle child, which came as a surprise to us all, and to this day, is a thorn of trauma & PTSD in my side. My daughter was diagnosed with Epilepsy in 2022. Well, kind of. She has never received an official diagnosis, her neurologists have been constantly running tests, doing exams, and other doctor things that I don't quite understand, to gain insight into exactly what she has and have been experiencing. The first night that we were aware of, that my daughter had a seizure, I think I felt my heart stop. I felt the world pause for a few minutes, and still to this day, I cannot pinpoint exactly how I felt at that moment. What was supposed to be a fun night out of the house ended up being one of the scariest nights of my life.

We decided on this night that since my youngest went with her dad for the weekend, my two older girls and I would find something fun to do, that fun thing ended up being that we were going to the bowling alley and arcade. I didn't really want to participate in the arcade games, so I opted to sit at the bar and have a drink, while the girls played in the arcade. This bowling alley is known in the area for having a lot of teen activity, which at times brought about teen fights and rambunctious behavior. As I sat at the bar, I did not think it strange that I saw security running in all different directions of the building. After a couple of minutes, I decided to call the girls' phone to make sure that they were okay. When I didn't get an answer from them, I still didn't think it to be strange as I assumed they must be playing and not able to hear their phone. I have good girls, and I have taught them that in the face of danger, you go in the opposite direction, plus they knew where to find me. As I sat and sipped on the alcoholic beverage I ordered, I wasn't sure if I was hearing things or if the drink was beginning to kick in, but I thought I heard my name on the loudspeaker to come to the front desk. I looked around, not sure if I heard that correctly or not, but as soon as I shook it off to ignore what I thought I heard, my oldest daughter was calling my phone. When I answered, I heard the urgency in her voice and immediately stood straight up like an erect statue. I ran through the building to every corner trying to find exactly where they were, when I reached where my daughters were, my oldest was being consoled by a friend and my middle child was lying on the floor, not moving. There was the arcade manager and a couple of other workers standing around her, along with a security guard keeping the crowd at bay.

I felt my knees buckle and I instantly hit the floor next to her, trauma response number one. I felt my entire body get hot, and a ringing began in my ear, I felt as though I was going to pass out right next to her on the floor. They would not allow me to touch her, so I didn't know if she was breathing or not. Was she dead? What the hell was happening? The manager informed me that the paramedics had been called and were on their way. That had to have been the longest fifteen minutes in history, it felt like an hour. My body was literally in shock, so much so to the point where I felt I was about to hyperventilate, I was sweating and my heart was racing, trauma response number two. As I kneeled next to her, there was still no sign of life to her, all I did was pray and continue to call her name and the Lord's.

"God please don't take her! Not now Lord. Cover my baby Jesus. Help my baby Lord! Give her back to me whole God. Please don't take her Jesus." That was all that I continued to say. I was crying so much because I just wanted to hug her, touch her skin, hold her and tell her that it was going to be okay, just like I did when she was two years old and fell down the brick steps at my mom's house and got a nosebleed. Or like the time my dad's dog, Trans, chased her around his auto shop and she ran yelling and crying to me. I so wanted to just say to her that everything was going to be okay, although I was not even sure that it would be.

When I saw my daughter's eyes begin to flicker, I yelled, "Thank you Jesus.," and in that same instant, the paramedics came rushing in with a stretcher. That may have just been another test. I think I passed that time. She was still very delirious and confused, she herself did not know what happened, as she was unconscious for almost thirty minutes. The medics began asking her sister, who was very shaken up, questions to better understand the cause, while there were another checking vitals. I wanted to know what had occurred as well, but I didn't want to overwhelm either one of the girls, so I kept my questions limited. In this moment, I knew that I just had to be mommy to them both.

Psalm 50:15, "and call upon me in the day of trouble; I will deliver thee, and thou shall glorify me."

The name of Jesus carries power. Calling on him brings forth the power and authority to save and heal. Because I believed, and called upon him in a time of trouble, I truly believe that I saved my daughter's life that night. The days and months that followed this traumatic night, I would find myself calling on him even more.

Following the night at the bowling alley, we had to undergo several doctor and hospital visits before we even had somewhat of a name for what my daughter was experiencing. The trauma and PTSD that followed caused me not to be able to sleep, because I constantly found myself walking to her bedroom in the middle of the night just to peek in and make sure that she was okay. When she took naps, I watched for the rhythm of her breathing to make sure that she was. I didn't allow her to lock the bathroom door when she showered or go anywhere without me nearby. I was so worried, as any mother would be. I could not understand how a child so sweet, so innocent, could endure such a thing. Why would God do this to her?

The more tests the doctors ran, the less answers we received. I was confused, and so were they. They gave a diagnosis on epilepsy, only because she was placed on aggressive seizure medication, because they had to prescribe something for her to be able to go back to school. The condition worsened, and became her having multiple seizures per day, and in the middle of the night while she slept. I became sleep deprived, amongst other things. The frustrations of not knowing gave me anxiety. I ended up being told by my job at the time that I was going to have to decide on what I was going to do about my position. It seemed, every time I arrived at work, within an hour I would have to leave because my oldest daughter would be calling to tell me that her sister had suffered yet another seizure while they were dressing for school. I ended up submitting my letter of resignation. This job that God had blessed me with, a government job, which paid well, one where I felt so important because I was able to obtain a secret security clearance to secure the position, was now snatched away from me. I blamed God.

This added trauma to being a mother was overwhelming and putting a huge dent in not only my finances, but my attitude. I found myself becoming so frustrated that I would lash these frustrations on the very people who depended on me. My children. I found myself venting to one of my best friends and informing her that I just didn't want to be a mother anymore, and that I hated my children. We all know I did not hate my children in real life; however, I hated the predicament we were in. I was strapped from the rootie to the tootie. The bills did not stop because I was unable to work or find a job that would accommodate my daughter's needs. I still had to be a mother, in my traumatic experience, I still had to tend to the things that were causing the trauma directly. Let's pause here, did you catch that?

Most times, when we are dealing with difficult situations, we rid ourselves of that thing.

A job we don't like, we find a new one. The car giving us trouble? We repair the issue or buy another one. Husband, or wife not doing right? We file for divorce. Hip joints causing us pain? We go to the doctor for physical therapy, meds, or surgery. The fact of the matter is, in most cases, when there is something bringing discomfort to our lives, we find a solution to get rid of or fix it. What do you do when the thing bringing discomfort is something that you still have to tend to?

What do you do, when the thriving of a thing is the very thing, you feel is killing you?

What do you do when you are in a literal chokehold, with no way to free yourself?

What do you do?

You probably shouldn't do what I did.

What I did caused more bad, than it did any good. I played the blame game. I blamed everyone, including my kids, for the way our life was. Looking back on those moments of vulnerability, where I had not known any better, makes me cry inside and outwardly. I made it their cross to carry when it was solely mine. I made my responsibilities theirs and guilted them into believing they were at fault. I was passing on trauma from trauma.

You know that saying, hurt people, hurt people. That was exactly what I was doing, I was allowing my battle scars to bleed onto my children, when they were not even responsible for the sword that caused the lacerations. This caused a wedge within our home. Our house was crumbling because the foundation, being myself, had.

At this time, I had already been in and out of therapy from dealing with my very burdensome and grueling divorce. Had I been using the proper side of my brain, I would have recognized that now would have been a better time than any to call my therapist and say, "Hey sis... fit me in expeditiously" I was losing my, excuse the French, shit! Don't gasp. I know some may have thought this book is my integration into ministry based on the title and how I am sure to promote it, but no. I still very much like to season my sentences with a minor cuss word here and there. God isn't through with me yet, but it's a start.

I found myself drenched in burden. I had begun to cause childhood trauma to my children. Though she never expressed it to me, my daughter felt at fault for my job situation. My children began to isolate themselves from me more and more. It was easier for them to stay locked away in their rooms, than to be out in our living space freely to hear me complain or fuss. I thank God for the quick revelation into what I was causing. Had I continued down the path, in ten or fifteen years you would probably be reading a book written by one of my kids telling how they overcame a traumatizing childhood.

We may not often realize how the things that we experience in life, be it big or small, truly do influence how we live life. Trauma doesn't just go away on its own, it will live with you and sometimes it will swell and one day you will have such an outburst from something that you didn't even realize was an issue for you. That is why healing is so important. Not just healing physically. Healing mentally and emotionally must occur as well. It is a continuous thing. I still have a therapist, and though I may not see her on a weekly basis as before, when I feel as if I am not myself and needing help, I call her, and we schedule accordingly. I will forever praise therapy! Growing up for many of us, I know it was not a thing.

Proverbs 15:22 "Without counsel, plans fail. With many advisors, they succeed."

Even the bible encourages us to seek counsel to assist us with our daily plans, such as living. Seek wise counsel! Meaning, a professional, not your girlfriend from across the street, or a nosy co-worker, but someone who is skilled and trained in how to assist others in navigating their feelings and emotions. You will see yourself as others see you, see the man or woman in the mirror.

This trauma has not since gone away, however, I am better at managing it. Sometimes, the trauma will never go away, but learning ways to deal with it and react in a better way is what helps keep it under control. Though my daughter has this diagnosis, we have not found it to be the end of it all for her or her life. She's a band kid and aspires to attend FAMU and join their band. While I was still under the control of the trauma, this was a no for me. Now that I am over control of the trauma, it could be a possibility. I sleep at night. I am not constantly waking to watch her in her bedroom while she sleeps. Every night before I go to bed, I pray!

I ask God to protect her, watch over her and provide rest, not just for her, but for all of us. Even my youngest makes sure that if I forget before she heads to bed, she will say to me, "Mom, we have to say our prayers."

My children have become accustomed to knowing that our prayers before bed at night are what is going to cover us and keep us protected while we sleep. This is the kind of thing that happens when you control the trauma and not allow the trauma to control you. It was a process. A lot had to happen prior to getting here. It took even first recognizing that something was even wrong. Being high strung, overwhelmed, and anxious all the time is not normal, and when I recognized that these things were in control of me, I sought help so that I could get back in control of it.

Remember what my grandmother would say about the happy bird? Well, ok then! You're learning.

It all begins with our thoughts, **Proverbs 23:7** "for as a man thinketh in his heart, so is he…"

Train your mind to think better, control your thoughts and everything else will follow it. You think trauma, you will be trauma. You think healing, you will be healed. Control the trauma, do not let the trauma control you!

IF ALL HEARTS ARE CLEAR...

Growing up in the A.M.E church, I had become accustomed to the repetitious saying towards the end of every service, "if all hearts are clear.", this would be stated by the pastor at the conclusion of the service as to let the parishioners know that there was nothing more to be said and the church service was ending. It was out of order if someone needed to give a last-minute announcement or testimony once this saying had been stated, you were looked at funny, because you knew better. The moans and groans from the others in the audience would showcase the mutual displeasure of your account by doing such.

I, however, used this saying in a different way. If you knew the Desiree that I was prior to my maturing and healing phase, then you know, I have never had a problem with clearing my heart. My grandmother used to say to us as children, to never hold any malice on your chest, because it could kill you. So, every opportunity that I had to let someone know how I felt, I took it, because, well, I didn't want to die early by holding it on my chest. I may have slightly misinterpreted what my grandmother may have meant by stating such, but one thing that is for certain, I'm not dead yet, so it must have worked. I find that we should all be "clearing our hearts" at some point or another. Mainly, finding a healthy outlet to relieve stress and take a deep breath when necessary. I realized not that long ago that my heart was not clear on many circumstances, it was the day that upon this realization, I ultimately died, not physically but, in a way, I did. I had promised myself that my heart would be cleared in one way or another. As a woman, and a woman who is sought as having class, outbursts and behaviors that are out of the norm are scrutinized. I had developed this "good girl" image in my latter years that was beginning to swallow me whole, just like the whale swallowed Jonah, or the new social media meme of T.D. Jakes asking to have you ever been swallowed up? I was. I was swallowed in the misery of keeping my mouth shut and playing nice. My mother would often say things to me like, "You're a public figure, act like it." Or "You have daughters now, don't embarrass them." The constant reminder to continuously remain in my good girl standings for the world, was swallowing the legend that once was Desiree, the sassy and outspoken. On the advice of those who seemed to care about how I was portrayed to the public, I began to shut my mouth, and not clear my heart so much. My mouthpiece in the past had been a deadly weapon, ripping and cutting off heads one by one. A two-edged sword with razor sharp edges sharp enough to split the famous Angel Oak Tree in half in less than five seconds. But I had to learn to keep it shut.

I shut my mouth when my ex-husband told the world that I was a bitter ex who kept him away from his child. This narrative was one that often caused me discord because what did he mean by I was keeping him away from his child, when I wanted nothing more than a consistent break from motherhood as often as I could. This was a constant back and forth between him and I, which ultimately resulted in me not having phone conversations with him. He had to text me so that I could keep a record of what he did and did not say. I was no longer interested in mutilating his ego in person, or by phone, which was far too easy. It was the first time I had realized that I was in fact dealing with a narcissist and habitual liar in real time. I had to learn to take caution, but I also developed the art of keeping my mouth shut with anything concerning him, it was not an easy thing to do by far, but I had found that it became necessary. The fuel to his fire was in my replies. The more I responded, the further into the sea of narcissism and manipulation he went. I had to shut my mouth when the proof that lay right within my iPhone could and would shut him down with a simple and easy quick upload to social media. However, I knew that my reward would be greater, if not soon, then definitely later. I shut my mouth, and I allowed these untruths to rip apart at my name like a lion feasting on a herd of Zebras for dinner. I hurt, but I shut my mouth, and my heart was not clear.

I shut my mouth when a previous boss at a company that I once worked for attempted to blackball me in stating that she did not approve of an action that was carried out by myself, when she ultimately did. I had text messages to prove it. I am the receipt Queen, so I keep some form of proof, it is how I have learned to deal with people who aren't always honest. This woman threw me under a bus, and had I not been in fear of losing my job at that time, and the little bit of income that I was receiving, I would have very well took my phone to the owner of the company's office and show him the many uncomfortable pictures that I received from my boss, who was a woman by the way, that very well would have surely provided me with a nice sized lawsuit settlement in court, enough to probably buy a house, car and put my kids through college. But I knew that my reward would be greater, if not soon, then definitely later. I decided to keep my mouth shut. My heart was not clear.

I shut my mouth when my mother and I had a conversation about a past occurrence, in which even still in that moment, she wanted me to give civility to my aggressor. She showed grace to a person that I had only wanted to see suffer, and she had expected me to do the same as she said, this was the will of God for us moving on. How on God's green earth did this woman want me to not only forgive, but also forget? Her ideology of the facts and mine did not match. I wanted to tell her so badly "Hell no! I will not.," but I wanted to keep the teeth that I had spent thousands on already for braces that still garnished unclosed spaces and a slight overbite. As much as I wanted to hold on and not let go, I knew that my reward was greater, if not soon, then definitely later. I kept my mouth shut. My heart was not clear.

I shut my mouth when I had learned of those that I called friends, had discussed things about me and my life in a group text, which had somehow leaked from the platform in which it was organized. I was shown proof of these very conversations that I disclosed with them in secret. My heart sunk, my mouth watered, and my anger rose, because these were people that I trusted with my life, with my children's lives. These people I confided in, these people I loved had betrayed me. I wanted so badly to say to them when they would hug and call me "sis" to back away or I would surely snatch them up and throw them into another dimension far away from me. I had to sit, eat, and sup with the Judas' of my life, as Jesus did when he was betrayed at the last supper. It was the most hurtful thing to know a thing and say nothing. Upon leaving their presence, I would cry my eyes out in frustration. The test in this moment was not loving and getting closer with God, but more so learning to still love my enemies despite my pain. This was new for me. Uncomfortable to say the least. However, I knew that my reward was greater, if not soon, then definitely later. I kept my mouth shut. My heart was not clear.

I shut my mouth as those who had never met me, never spoken a word to me or with me, judged me from things told by others. Everyone had an agenda to scandalize Desiree. To this day it is not understood, as I have always felt that I was the type of person that would give the shirt off my back to a stranger, had I a shirt to give, yet, my name was being tarnished, my image was being stomped on, my character was being judged and my social media pages were being monitored and picked apart for clues or insight into my life. I found this to be more comical than hurtful, as I never knew I would ever be such an interesting topic of conversation, I found my own life to be pretty basic and monotonous however, there were some who found entertainment in everything that I did or said. To keep myself from causing drama where there had to be none, I chose to ignore these desperate attempts for a group chat topic. I knew that by doing so, my reward would be greater. If not soon, then definitely later. I shut my mouth. My heart was not clear.

I shut my mouth because I did not want to be deemed problematic and add any fuel to the fire on the list of things that were already being said about me. This had become a trying point in my life because I was so used to setting people straight concerning me, I never had a problem getting it off my chest, but God had me in a different space. I could constantly hear him say to me that this battle was not mine to fight. I had at this point, been reading the bible more and familiarizing myself with the characters in the bible. I was now comparing myself to the greatest of the greats within the book that too had been scandalized, yet God availed them in the end. I assumed that if I just remained quiet and continued this journey of positivity and healing and maturing, that soon, all truth would come to light and my prayers would reach heaven, and vengeance would be mine. I realized that I had to become okay with the things that were being fabricated concerning me, enough to the point that it did not bother me. That was a very hard thing to do. Most times, as humans, we often feel it necessary to defend our name, and not allow anyone to tarnish that, for some, our names are all that we have. Why would we allow anyone to spew negative things concerning us and not say or do anything to vindicate ourselves? I learned the hard way that it was not my duty to address anything, because my name was just that, a name. My name, although as beautiful as it is, did not make me the person that I am, it only identified me. Whew, did you catch that? That is a word!!

The identification of the name Desiree, French for "to desire," only gave recognition to the person that either stood, sat, or mingled among the crowd with others. It did not, however, give any insight into my character, whether old or new, nor did it outwardly inform anyone of the changes that had taken place within my mind, my body, my spirit, and my heart. To clear my heart, was to ultimately not allow it to be troubled, or broken by anyone or anything. This was not an overnight action; it was not even a thirty-day action or a ninety-day action. This took years. Years of simply just shutting up!

I remember, when I was a little girl, I had joined my mom on an outing with a girlfriend of hers. I was never allowed to mix in adult conversations, or outings, however, this time, I believe my mom had no choice as she was not able to find a babysitter on this day. I quietly listened and soaked in the grown-up conversation, as she and her friend talked, feeling a little bit more mature as the day went on, I felt like I was one of the big girls for a day. As my mom and her friend continued their not so private discussion, my little ears perked up when my mom began to fabricate an occurrence to her friend. It was something simple, her just simply stating why she was unable to attend a previous outing that the friend had invited her on. I vividly remembered my mom forfeiting this event with her friend, because once before, listening in on one of her adult conversations, I remembered her telling her sister, "I ain't feel like all that bunch of running around. She forever wanna go out to them people house, and I don't mix up like that."

As I heard my mom so quickly dish out this lie, I was at first intrigued. I thought grown-ups couldn't tell lies, well, at least she always made it a point to tell me not to tell a fib, but here she was, telling one with the straightest face that she could. I took it upon myself to interject. I thought that my mom had forgotten what she had told her sister, so I thought it was my duty to help her to remember. In the instant that I placed myself in this conversation that was not for me, the glare that my mom gave me as she turned around to look at me from the front seat of the car, made me realize that I had just messed up big time. I want to say something else, but, you know, you all are thinking this is a Christian book, so I shall not deter your assumptions and thoughts. I saw the flames of hell within my mother's eyes, I saw my short little life flash before my eyes, I knew I was in trouble. My mom yelled out "Shut the hell up! You talk too damn much! Learn to just shut up sometimes."

I want to let my mother know, because I am sure that she will read this book, as she reads all my publications, Mom, I learned to shut the hell up. It may have taken me several years, but I did it girl! Thank you for directing me to do so.

Silence can be golden. In my season of shutting up, I became more observant. I noticed things and people that I probably hadn't before, because I was always talking, always clearing off my chest. For as many people there were that were against me, I learned that there were far more that were not. I had a plethora of people that were inspired by me and my life, as raggedy as I felt it was. I began to notice them. There were people that saw good in me, that supported me, that loved me and would speak kind of me to others, and I noticed them. Because I had finally learned to shut up, God began to reveal to me, the people that mattered. People with kindred souls that matched my own. People without an agenda, those that genuinely cared and loved, I noticed them. He gave me discernment and showed me that it was okay to open up to them.

There were people that I used to tell everything to, couldn't wait to call or text them to tell them what had happened to me, whether it was something good or something bad. In my silence, I realized that when these people knew nothing, the world knew nothing. Strange how that happens isn't it. Once I shut up and gave no information about myself to those, I thought were friends, the rumors no longer spread, the drama no longer found me, my name was not being called. My character and who I truly was on the inside was now being discussed, my name was now only being used to identify the character of who I was. My shutting up season became my vengeance. I didn't have to fight back; I didn't have to battle with anyone concerning my name. I did not have to clear my chest off on anyone, because I found the good in just shutting up sometimes. My vision became clearer because my mouth was no longer doing excessive work, the bible tells us in **Matthew 26:41** "watch and pray so that you will not fall into temptation." It does not say anything about speaking! It says to watch, you can't watch if you are always talking, then, pray. Shut up. Watch. Pray. Got it? Good. Now, if all hearts are clear!

I FEEL IT

I probably cannot pinpoint the exact day, or hour that I knew I was a different person. I just knew that things that I used to do, I wasn't doing anymore. Places that I used to go; I had no interest in going there anymore. People that I used to be around; I had no interest in hanging around them. I thought I was in a stage of depression because it was not normal, and I could not explain it. I blamed God, because of all this good that I was trying to do, he was causing me to isolate myself more and more from the things and people that I loved. I blamed him for making me like this, and now people were going to think that I was acting funny. That was sure to cause more whispers and ugly stares. Now God, I can barely handle the shutting up phase and not clearing my chest on folks enough as it is, just give me more reason to have to fight for my life even more. I felt like he was up there in heaven getting a good chuckle out of my confusion.

I felt new, but still old and raggedy if that makes any sense to you. It was like, I wanted to fully embrace this new person, but I felt obligated to remain with those from my previous life, because they had not wronged me in ways to warrant a departure of socialization. It was not the fact of leaving them behind, but more so, accepting that I was leaving the old version of me behind. It was not about them; it was about me. Because I felt like a new person, and was ultimately becoming a new person, I had to accept my new person, and until I did, God could not and would not move fully in my life as he so desired. He allowed me breadcrumbs into the life that awaited me, had I just given it all to him and allowed him to move freely within me.

I did not want to do that. I wanted to still have remnants of old Desiree, I liked her. She was fun, and carefree. She lived life on the edge without a care as to who thought what. Old Desiree was always a vibe. When she entered the room, people paid attention. She was okay with being herself, not having to pretend to be anything or anyone else, and I loved that about her. Did I love old Desiree, more than I loved my devotion to God?

That was a question that I had to continuously ask myself during this transition. Of course, my answer was always no, but my actions proved different. It wasn't what I was saying, but more so what I was doing. I was straddling the fence, hot minute and cold the next. I felt lost. Still, as I was trying very hard to maneuver this spiritual journey towards being a better individual, of all the progress that I had made, I was still lost. Dammit! Why did this have to be so hard? I felt I was already doing enough. I blamed God!

The worse kind of Christian to be is probably the lukewarm Christian. I think he would prefer us to either be all in or all out. Same as I feel about people that I encounter daily. Don't half deal with me, either you are going to be with me, or against me, but whichever you choose, stand on that! I feel like God wants the same. Being a devout Christian is tough, I don't think that I could ever be fully ready and prepared for all that the life of such entails. For goodness sakes, I can recite about thirty cuss words per minute, it flows like water from my lips. You mean to tell me that I would have to just cold turkey stop seasoning my sentences?

Yes. That was exactly what that meant. Now, for those of you that still follow me, just know, God is not through with me yet. It's a tricky process, but one that I have humbly accepted. It's a journey. It is imperative though, that within this walk, that we choose to be and do right. I do not want this to sound like a sermon, I am not preaching, nor am I 100% either, but we are reminded in the word of this.

2 Corinthians 6:17-18 "therefore, come out from among them and be ye separate, saith the Lord, and touch not the unclean thing; and I will receive you, and will be a Father to you, and ye shall be my sons and daughters, saith the Lord Almighty."

This was the instructions he had given to the Israelites after they had been freed from slavery. He wanted them to maintain their purity by not touching the forbidden things or dwelling in those spaces. He desires us to live in freedom from sin. No, we are not perfect people, however, being all in and fully devoted to him will help in assuring that the separation from the unclean remains consistent. We have all been lukewarm, I am probably just a few degrees above being lukewarm. Being lukewarm causes spiritual lethargy and stunts our growth from what we are trying to overcome. Others will look at you and know you from your past, and they will say that you have not changed. They will say that you are the same and that God has not transitioned you. This is why daily prayer is necessary, you must proclaim daily that you are new, you are devoted and that you are changed. **Isaiah 43:19** "Behold, I will do a new thing, now it shall spring forth, shall ye not know it? I will even make a way in the wilderness, and rivers in the desert."

Imagine yourself as the desert. Imagine you, dried up, barren, no sign of life. When he is doing a new thing in your life, he will break down strongholds, transform your dark spaces into light, soften your heart, open your ears and eyes, he will feed you when you hunger, clothe you when you are naked, give water when you thirst, provide you with hope and faith to continue another day, in him!

That was what I felt. In my barren and dry state. He did a new thing. He provided springs of water to my soul. Where there was once barren land, now flourished greenery and scenic land. When I was thirsty, he gave me water. He gave me hope and faith. I felt new. I felt nourished. I felt free! Even more than I had before, I thought I was free to be me, when in actuality, I was caged because I felt that I had a perception to upkeep. That was not freedom, that was bondage. The more I took this journey, the more my eyes became opened to the things that I did not clearly see before. I feel it. I feel me. I feel different. I feel new. I feel it. I feel…. God!

JUST A LITTLE TALK

I don't think that I will ever fully become comfortable with talking to God and having him to talk back. I like it better when he lets me do all the talking and replies to me in a dream or something. That first experience almost took me out of here, straight up heart attack!
I have come to find that I enjoy talking to him and knowing now that he hears me. I never felt that he did before. All my blame was put on him because I was not on the level that I needed to be to hear him although he was talking all along.

When I was a little girl, maybe around the age of twelve or thirteen, my mom had purchased a green dodge caravan. We lived out in the country, so it was not out of the norm to open the sliding door to the van, and crash inside the van playing with my dolls, listening to music or something while my mom and brothers tended to the yard work. We had a huge yard, so that job would sometimes take hours, but it felt good to sit back in the breeze while my mom and siblings worked. One evening, my older brother Eliot joined me in the van to take a break from all the yard work that my mom had him doing. As he lay stretched out on the floor of the van, I said to him, "I want to go to the store and get some candy and a juice.," now, I did not have a permit, or a driver's license. In fact, I was still a few years off from being able to obtain either. Maybe my brother thought that I had been joking around, but I was serious about wanting some snacks from the store, he said to me "Well, go ahead. The keys are right there."

Sure enough, the keys to my mom's new van were right in

the ignition. So, I crawled behind the steering wheel, and cranked the van. When I put the van in gear, thinking I had put it in drive, when I had actually put it in reverse, my brother sat straight up like a mummy in a coffin. Before he could catch his footing to run out of the van, I had already mashed the gas. The van crashed into a tree in the yard and we both darted out of the van, with the engine still running and the van still in gear, towards the house yelling "Mama! Mama!," because we both wanted to be the first to tell on the other. Though my brother did not crank the van, put it in gear or mash the gas, he was equally responsible for giving me the permission to do so, I felt that he too was to blame. I don't remember what our punishments were for the occurrence, it's probably something traumatic that I have pushed away from my memory. I never felt that I was wrong in this situation, to this day, my brother tells this story in his version, and I tell it in mine, as adults, we still blame the other for being at fault. Honestly, I don't know who was to blame, my brother for giving me the authority to drive knowing that I couldn't, or myself for even cranking the ignition and taking the chance. This was how I felt during of my confused occurrences with God. Was he to blame for allowing me to walk into a thing, because he knew what the outcome would be before I had even executed the action. Or was this all the fault of my own because I was the one that carried out the action?

Imagine, receiving blame for something that you did not authorize. My blame to God was just that. He did not authorize me to do any of the things that was causing my demise, but because I was too far away from him to even hear his direction clearly, or even understand his will for my life, I blamed him for the things that he was ultimately trying to protect me from. His will and mine did not match, and this in fact caused me to stray further away from him because I didn't think he cared.

The failed marriages, the stress of single motherhood, the rape, the molestation, the financial struggles, the jail sentence (yes, I have been to jail before... though I very rarely discuss, it happened), the mental struggles, the emotional struggles, all of it, I blamed God.
The more I began to open my heart to him, talk to him and accept him, the more I was able to hear him. My grandmother and my Aunt Mary would often sing a song in church that went...
"Let us, have a little talk with Jesus, tell him all about our troubles, he will, hear our faintest cry, and answer by and by, when you, feel the little prayer wheel turning, and you know that the fire is burning, let us, have a little talk with Jesus makes it right, alright." If you know anything about the old southern church, the mothers would swing up and down the aisles during this song, someone would beat a tambourine while the rest of us hand clapped and input that double hand clap that you only hear the right way down in the south. This song had meaning, it had purpose and it held truth.
I found that just a little talk with him was making things right after all. He answers when he is called, when he is sought after, he will make himself visible to you. There are several instances in the bible where one spoke to God, and he answered and made things right. Moses, when he spoke to the burning bush. Abraham, Solomon, David, Esau, Samuel, and several others. My confusion was knowing when he spoke and what he was saying versus me just having a thought.

I used to think that God talking to me required a face-to-face conversation, much like what I would have with an ordinary person day to day. When I would sit in church and hear the speaker preaching or prophesying saying, they heard God. I would sit in doubt, like "Yeah right! If you can hear him, I should be able to hear him too if he's in the room."
My doubt was actually fear. Most times, we fear what we don't understand, so we cast doubt.
What would I have done had I heard him for myself, especially being in such a lost state spiritually that I was at that time? How would I have reacted to a voice so strong, yet soft at the same time? What would I have done, if I knew that it was the creator of all things speaking directly to me, an omnipresent being that was revered by all, talking to me, how would I have accepted that?

It was not until I began my personal spiritual journey, and tapped into what he was doing, that I began to recognize the gift that I had been given. Now, this is going to sound crazy to some, yet very relatable to others. I am a Seer, a dreamer, and a visionary, in today's terms, we call these people prophets. I do not consider myself as such in today's understanding of what a prophet is. I do not publicize this for two reasons, I have not even fully been able to tap into this gift as I should and I know how I feel about some people that claim to be "prophets", I don't question anyone's relationship with God, but a part of my gift is having discernment to know who and what is real. However, I have had encounters and things I have seen and sometimes even felt before it even happened. It may have come as a dream, I'd think nothing of it and a few weeks later, the very thing I had dreamed would be playing out right before my eyes. I have had visions, in which I would see a thing happening and within a few days that very vision would occur. I have had feelings, or thoughts and those same thoughts and feelings would happen. At first, I assumed it was a coincidence that these things occurred, maybe I just, I don't know, had a "by chance" moment. I never thought that it was a gift, or a curse, just something that happened. It was not until I was listening to an interview that Tabitha Brown was doing on YouTube. She was talking about her gift, of being a dreamer and a Seer and how she hears God's voice. What she was explaining was exactly what I had experienced and been feeling. It was also confirmation of her book, because I had read her book, "Feeding the Soul," the year before I heard this interview, so it took me back to what I had read. What was crazy about the time I heard this interview, was because around this time, I was asking God to help me to understand why these things were occurring. Also, during this time, when I heard the interview, I was also reading Cicely Tyson's book, "Just as I Am," and she too was talking about her gift of having visions and dreams. I then began to think, wait a minute! So, I am not crazy, and it is not just me. Famous people were having these same occurrences that I was having assuming them to be just by happenstance.

I wanted to understand this gift. I was intrigued. I wanted to know more, so I began to research and find more insight into what this was exactly. That was a moment of God speaking to me, because I had questions, he provided me with answers in the form of Tabitha's interview and Cicley's book. It was like he was saying, "Here you go! There is your answer, now what?" I won't get too much into my gift of being a Seer, a dreamer and visionary, because I do not want anyone to misunderstand my gift, because like I said, I have yet to understand it. Maybe I will write another book about it in the future, because it has been quite an experience for sure.

The point is, talking with God provides answers. How to recognize his voice depends on how well you decide to pay attention, and whether you choose to listen. Through our circumstances, dreams, a feeling, music, a tv show, an interview, a book, thoughts, and visions, all of these are answers from God when we talk to him and ask him questions. How do you recognize his voice? That takes knowing him. Get closer with him, spend time with him. Familiarize yourself with his words. Read and study!

Have just a little talk with him, tell him all that you desire to know, and be consistent with him.
Just a little talk with Jesus makes it right, ALRIGHT.

RENEWED

To be renewed means to change into something new and different, something better. In order to feel different and be different, you have to do different things. I would often proclaim being a child of God, but actually provoked no actions to prove that I was. I wasn't tithing, wasn't reading the bible, praying or even going to church. I was talking about it, but not being about it, and I felt I had my reasons. I didn't think that it was necessary to do any of the above, because if I said that I am what I am, that was enough for me to believe that I was and should have been enough for the world too.

That's where we become trapped. One of the main reasons why many people, myself included stray or have strayed from the church, or the fold of a spirituality and a having a relationship with God, is because we hear with our own ears, so many proclaim to be the holiest of holies, yet their actions prove much different. I experienced it, I lived with one of the same, and I too saw with my own eyes and heard with my own ears the fallacy of the wretched ones. I told myself that there was no way in hell, that God could be real. Such a perfect God would create these beings.

People that proclaimed to love and serve him with their whole hearts, and two steps out of the church door were sinning more than sin could sin itself. God, these your chirrin'? There was no way that I was going to put my faith and trust in a God that allowed that. Maybe I should write another book called, "Secrets Beyond the Pulpit", because honey let me tell you something, I have seen and experienced somethings within the four walls of a church and with those who reign in the highest of the most highs of accolades and titles within several different denominations. However, this book isn't that, maybe some other time. The point is these were some of the very experiences that contributed to my going astray. Not just mine, but others as well. I remember my oldest brother trying to explain to my mother once over the dinner table why he refused to attend church. This was blasphemy in my mother's house, for the obvious reason, she was a preacher. How could the preacher's kid not want to go to church?

His reasoning was simple and valid. He stated to my mother, why would he go to church to listen to the same preacher preach to the congregation about living right and not doing bad things, when this same preacher was one that was drinking and smoking weed along with him under the neighborhood trees with the other older gentlemen that he hung out with often. My mother, stunned, had no words. She had no explanation to give. With that, she never asked my brother about coming to church ever again, and I have never seen my brother step foot into one other than for a funeral. Many feel this way, and I very much dislike to hear the church people say, "We all sin and fall short" or, "there is no room for judgment, only God can judge.," where is the accountability? I always felt this was a cowardly excuse to not have to be accountable for their actions. Yet, let one that was not within the fold of God do something just as equal to their sin, the phones of the gossiping church hens would be ringing off the hook to dish the tea.

It was well into my adulthood, and when I say well into, I mean like a couple of years ago, that I realized that my faith and relationship with God could not be based on what I saw from others. The truth of the matter is, none of us are perfect beings and if I was depending on the folks that I knew within the church to get me into heaven, we would all be going to hell in a gasoline drenched handbasket with gasoline drenched underwear and wigs on. Some of the very people that we reverence, are the ones committing adultery, fornicating, lusting, stealing, scamming and all kinds of other things that The Ten Commandments tells us not to do, but that is between them and their God, not mine. I learned that I had to be stronger than those around me, I had to fight harder because I truly wanted this, I wanted a closer relationship with God, but I was not going to get it by watching someone else's plate. I had to be renewed, and I had to go through this renewal of my mind, my heart, and my soul, daily.

I had to renew my knowledge, my attitude, my mind, my strength, and my spirit if I desired to truly be a new being. This was a must for me daily and still is! Imagine what we are faced with every day as soon as we leave our homes. The kids moving slow and not wanting to wake up for school, now here I go cussing everybody out. Traffic bad, nobody wants to drive as though they actually have someplace to be, I'm cussing again. Baby daddy lying about why the child support check is late, yup, there goes another cuss word. Another bill due by the end of the day tomorrow, when I just paid the last one yesterday late, another cuss word slips. It became of the upmost importance for me to renew myself constantly while I set forth to seek living a life that reflects Christ.

Romans 12:2 "Do not conform to the pattern of this world but be transformed by the renewing of your mind."

2 Corinthians 4:16 "For which cause we faint not; but though our outward man perish, yet the inward man is renewed day by day."

I wanted to be better, I wanted to be different. The renewing began with me first. I had to first make the decision that I was even going to do it. Then, I made sure to begin to pray and ask God for guidance to help me to stay on the path I had set out to be on. I wanted to also make sure that once I started, that I wasn't going to be deterred by the things I had seen and known by other so-called Christians, so, as much as this pained me in some instances, I had to limit my relationships with those that did not live a life pleasing to what I was seeking. I joined a new church. I stopped sitting on the phone and gossiping about church business, and with church people. If there were things that I was aware of, that I know was not pleasing to God, I excused myself from those people, those places and most of those actions. I wanted no parts.

I could I renew daily, yet still do the same things, or hang around the same people. It's like having a glass of water in a contaminated cup, you pour that water from that cup into a filter to be purified, yet, from the filter, the water is poured back into the same contaminated cup. There is just no purpose in filtering the water. I wanted to be like purified water, but I wanted my cup to be clean. The most important part of this decision was knowing that I owed no one an explanation for my absence. Feel what you feel, think what you think, I know the journey that I am on and why. I know what I have been told, and I know what God showed me. I also know that most will not accept the change, because they are stuck in my previous years. Some people will only see and know you for who you were, not for who you are, or for who you will be, and that, my God told me, is okay. No one is supposed to see a vision that was not given to them. It is yours and yours alone, again I say, your relationship and walk with God will always be personal.

As I continue to write this book, I am in the very early stages of my renewal and my journey. Even by the completion of this book, I cannot say that I would have reached where I desire to be, but I know that I will be just a few steps further along from where I am today. I may backslide, I may fall, I may lose a time or two, and all those things are okay, they are bound to happen. It's more so what I will do with the "getting up", that will demand God's attention.

Isaiah 40:31 "but they that wait upon the Lord, shall renew their strength; they shall mount up with wings as eagles; they shall run and not be weary, they shall walk and not faint."

I have begun walking this journey to be educated, to be inspired, to be closer to one, but for a short time and I do not feel tired. I am renewed.

IT AIN'T OVER

My grandmother and great-aunts and uncles used to scare me so much as a child, when they would sit on my grandmother's back porch, eating peanuts or sliced apples talking about the end of the times. "God, why would you just put me here and then so quickly snatch me away, I am just a little girl.," I would think to myself while I listened to their conversations. I would wander around the yard afterwards, just thinking to myself that at any moment, rapture would come, the trumpets of the Lord would sound, the angels would descend and within an instant, my tiny little earthly life would be over.

As I grew older, and attended more church services, my anxiety would rise when the preacher would announce to the congregation, "We don't have much time left, get right with God, and get right with him now."
True indeed, none of us know the time, day nor even the hour. But will it really all be over?
What is truly the end of a thing?

I have prided myself lately on living my life as though it will be my last day.
I started a thing in 2023, right before my birthday, although I was on this journey of being a new being and having a more intentional life, right before I turned thirty-seven, I was

feeling quite stuck. I felt stuck in motherhood, stuck in my job at the time, just waking up every day and doing the same routine. It made me unhappy in a sense. The weekend before my birthday, I woke up at 5:30am, and as much as I tried to roll over to go back to sleep, I just could not. I figured I would go to the gym in my apartment community, so I got up, showered, and threw on my gym clothes. Instead of walking the short distance over to the gym, I somehow ended up packing clothes in a bag. I questioned this unorthodox action, and I asked God, "What is this you're doing?"

I sat back down on my bed once I had fully packed my bag, confused. Then, like fresh wind, I heard, "Go travel and release."
I woke my two oldest daughters up, my youngest was with her father for the weekend, and told them to pack a bag, we were going out of town.

This very impromptu trip was not in my budget for the week, in fact, it would very much cut into the money that I set aside for my rent for the upcoming month, but it was almost as though I was not even the one in control of my own body within that moment. My daughters got packed and dressed, and within an hour I had gassed up my car and we were on the road, but to go where?
As we drove through town and made it to the interstate, I said to them, "Where would you like to go?" Neither of them said a word, they just looked at me. I could tell by the confused look on their faces that they were still trying to grasp my abrupt wake up and pack up. They both reared back in the seats of the car and decided to go back to sleep. I was left alone, driving nowhere. When I reached the fork in road in Columbia, I could either continue straight, or go to the

right, going right would take me to Charlotte, I figured, that maybe a nice trip. But then remembered the big Dallas Cowboys and Carolina Panthers game that was taking place that same weekend, so I said to myself, "Naw, hotels will be hard to find, and the city will be crowded.," so I continued to drive straight. After a few minutes, I said, "I will just drive to Greenville, I like Greenville and then I can see Anaya and Buddy.

Anaya is my oldest niece, my heartstring for sure, and Buddy is her one-year-old baby boy, whom I adore. I don't get the opportunity to see either of them often, as my niece is currently bogged down in nursing school, so usually when there is freedom in both our schedules, I will go visit her.

This was the quietest car ride on a road trip ever. I did not even turn the music on. As the girls slept, I felt like silence was needed. My thoughts began to fill my mind, and I knew within this moment, that God was talking to me. As I drove, I saw visions. I saw visions of what was to come if I continued to follow a specific path. I saw me, my children, and others around us, some whom I had not yet even met at this time, and I saw us all happy, glowing, and basking in the joys of life. Things that I had recently been asking God for in prayer, was being revealed to me as I drove in silence.

I was disturbed out of my vision by a loud noise coming from beneath my vehicle.

I thought to myself, "Not a flat tire!!" as that was exactly what it had seemed it was. I pulled off at the next exit, into a gas station. Not wanting to alarm the girls, because a flat tire would surely set this trip back, not only timewise, but also financially as money was already tight just to be on this unexpected adventure. I got on all fours and looked underneath the car at all four of my tires, nothing. Not one tire was flat, nothing was hanging from underneath the car, and I saw nothing that would alarm me that there was an issue. After a quick bathroom break, we were back on the road, closer to our destination.

There were no plans made once we arrived in Greenville but being that my birthday was just a few short days away, I told the girls that there was only one thing that I wanted to do, which was also my most favorite past time and hobby, and that was to visit a winery. I have this desire, this dream to one day be in the wine industry, I have what I think is one of the greatest ideas for a wine business that I have only told three people, and one that I cannot tell you in this book, as there is no way for me to have you sign an NDA, however, if the Lord sees fit, I pray that he will bless me with what I will need to move forth. I love wine, not just the taste of it, but the luxury of just being a wine connoisseur girlie. Pairing wine with different meals, going to wineries, and learning about different grapes, all of it, I just enjoy it so much.
We found a nice, and quant winery on the backroads of Greenville and made it our first stop. I enjoyed this little piece of heaven so much. There was an area outside near a wineglass shaped lake, with chairs and a small little water fountain. We sat out there, now with my niece and my Grandnephew in attendance and allowed the sun to reign down on us while we just talked, laughed, took photos, and let Buddy run around in the grass. This was joy. For me, this was all that I needed on this day. I was at so much peace and happiness at just this simple little thing. This was exactly what I needed. The stagnant unhappiness that I had been feeling while at home instantly vanished. Being in nature, and with a few of the ones I loved most, did my heart good.

It was like God was saying to me, "Enjoy the simple things in life, this is where your happiness resides."

The entire weekend was spent just as the first day. There was no itinerary. I had no plans to really do anything special, but everything that we did was enjoyable, it was peaceful, fresh, free and I felt love. My heart felt light, and my mind was not consumed with what was happening back home. I enjoyed it so much that I began to do these impromptu trips more often. No plans, just get up and go, and it didn't have to be anywhere special, just for some time to feel that same feeling that I felt on that weekend, I yearned for it more and more.

A couple of days after I arrived back home from the weekend trip to Greenville, as a matter of fact, it was the day after Thanksgiving, Black Friday. My car made that weird noise again, the same noise I had heard while on the road to Greenville, but this time, it was worse. I was only a mile or two down the street from my apartment, so I opted to continue to drive about ten miles per hour until I made it safely into my complex. I again got on all fours, looked underneath the car, and saw nothing. I called my brother, who was now the family mechanic since my dad passed and told him what had occurred. A day or two later, he came over to examine the car and towed it into another repair shop not far from where I lived. The old man that was working on the car, came into the lobby of the auto shop and proclaimed loudly, "Who's the owner of the white maxima?", embarrassed as to what his next statement would be, I shyly lifted my hand to let know that I was the owner.
"Come outside ma'am, we need to talk."

I followed him into the bay where my car was hoisted up high on a lift. He walked me around all sides underneath the vehicle and showed me all the issues that I had. My car was in bad shape. In the shorter version of our conversation, he basically told me that my car's tires, wheel bearings, axle, struts, basically everything needed to maneuver the car were so bad that he was surprised that I hadn't been in an awful wreck. Though my four tires were fairly new, they were practically shredded to pieces on the inner side. He showed me how loose the bearings were, where the axle was practically hanging, the struts and all kinds of other mechanical jargon that I don't recall. He saw a car seat in the back, which belonged to my youngest and looked at me and said, "You ride kids in this car?"

I wanted to burst out in laughter, because y'all know that I am the most unserious person ever, I love a little chuckle. But I smiled and said, "Yes sir. Three girls."

When I looked back over at him, I realized he did not find any humor in my response. He simply stated, "Yall could have died. Your lives would have been OVER!"

After sitting there for hours while the main things were repaired so that I could at least get back on the road and scheduling an appointment to get the other things repaired. The one thing that continued to replay in my mind was the mechanics statement, "your lives would have been over."

I drove that car all the way to Greenville and back. Not to mention, around town, and back and forth to my mom's house during the Thanksgiving holiday. God, you took me there and back, and all-around town with my vehicle in this condition, and you did it safely?

Later that night, I could not sleep. I got up and wrote in my journal about the ordeal, and how I thanked God so much for keeping us safe. I thought about what would happen with Taylor, if her sisters and I did get into a car accident on that road trip and die. My mind flashed to how sad everyone would be, losing me and my two oldest daughters. I envisioned Facebook posts from my closest friends, sympathizing at how I had died right before my thirty-seventh birthday. My mind was stuck in the realm of grief of what could have been, so much so, until tears began to roll down my face, and the rhythm of my heartbeat became brisk. My mind took me back to the conversations my grandmother had on her porch with her siblings about our last days, them all being passed on now, I envisioned meeting them at the gates. My Uncle John with his bucket hat that he always wore. My grandmother Mag, with her favorite housedress on and surely a pot or broom in her hand as she was always cooking or cleaning. My Aunt Maudie, with her beautiful silky hair and her pretty curls, and my Uncle Norton, with his cane and thick coke bottle glasses. This vision provided me with their images, just as clear as if they had been standing right in front of me. I could hear my grandmother laughing and saw my Uncle John laughing back with her. My Aunt Maudie, always having been a sweet woman, offering me her hand as if she was ushering for me to come along and join them.
Within that same instant I saw my father pop into the frame, leading me back outside of the gate, saying, "Babygirl, it ain't over."

Once I was able to shake what I was experiencing, I was in a full-on fit of grief. My dad's death is still very much a sore spot for me. My mind had led me to this place, where I did not even have to go, because I had survived the very thing that could have been a reason for my demise. There wasn't even an accident. I got so angry, with myself and with God, because why was I experiencing these things? Why would it make me so sad?

I have never told anyone about these experiences, as I stated in the previous chapter, I have not yet been able to tap into this gift, though I am aware it is a gift. There are times that I don't even want it. I want to be normal; I don't want to be more special than what I already am, especially not as whatever witchy, spiritual being these visions and dreams were causing me to be. I do not want it. Once I had gotten myself together, stopped crying and being enraged. I knelt beside my bed to pray. I figured that being mad at God wasn't going to change his mind, so I prayed to him to help me to understand and furthermore, to have peace. Peace that would surpass my understanding, so that I could accept whatever this was.

I know that those who may feel they know me on a more personal level know me as Desiree that takes no stuff, will tell you off, will make jokes about serious situations, some call it dark humor, and one who loves her children. I make no refutes to any of those claims, however, I would urge you all to know the Desiree that I am now. Know the Desiree that is on a journey, one that she is fully endowed to completing. Know the Desiree that has done so much inner work to be a renewed being. Know the Desiree that is at peace with all things and all people. Know the Desiree that would rather exit a situation or a conversation, versus indulging in any obscenities. Know the Desiree that does not want to hear any gossip. Know the Desiree that will write you off quickly if you do not respect her boundaries. Know the Desiree that is just on a path to live a more purposeful life, and if you intend to be a part of that life, you must be just as purposeful and intentional with your words and actions as I am.

It's a journey, it won't happen right away, or overnight. When God puts something in your spirit, and your heart, he won't allow you to rest until you embrace. He will keep talking to you, he will keep making you uncomfortable and he will keep sending you the signs until you accept what it is he is trying to do. Some people die never ever living or even knowing their purpose. Imagine how whole you will be by being one of the few people that not only knows your purpose but lives it as well. It will do your heart so much good. My journey is not yours and yours will not be mine but know that when you are a purpose filled individual, one with a calling to God's people, your "I won't give up" game will be strong. You may not understand it either. I remember wanting to die and couldn't. I asked, "God, how come every time these bad and horrible things happen to me, I just get up and keep going? I'm tired!" He won't allow it. He will not allow you to quit. He has work for you to do, and until you accept that he does, and until you do that work which he set forth for you to do, it ain't over until God says it's over!

I STILL BLAME GOD

Playing the blame game was easy, because it did not require me to have to take accountability for my shortcomings. If God had in fact, not liked me, as I had thought, and was purposely inflicting these hardships onto me, then why would he have given me any sort of immunity to still have the chance to turn my thoughts around and do things differently?

My spirit was given another chance to be renewed and restored. When we experience that, we experience an outpouring of God's love and assurance. The renewal and restoration of our minds, gives us more perspective of God and what his possibilities are for our lives. It provides us with the tools we need to maintain our faith and remain anchored in the word of God. I don't know what many may have thought that this book was going to be about. I wrestled with the idea of the title, I even wrestled with the idea of writing it, because this journey is still so very new and fresh for me. People can sometimes be so judgmental and mean. I did not want anyone to deter me from my path, by me publicly giving information about my most sacred self for the world to judge and murmur about. I thought, at one point, that maybe I would just write these thoughts down in my journal. Once I had reached a level in my spirituality where I would be comfortable, then I could look back on these words to see just how far I had come. I also thought that if anything happened to me and my life came to an end for some reason, these words would one day emerge either by either one of my daughters, or someone so intrigued by my life that they would find it and decide to publish it so that the world would know the late, yet great, Desiree Middleton.

When I was in middle school, I read the book, "The Diary of Anne Frank," a young girl who was trapped in an attic for two years along with her family during the Nazi invasion of the Netherlands. This is still one of my most favorite books to date. Somehow, I always saw myself as Anne Frank in some ways. Trapped in plain sight. Hidden, but not afraid. Secretive, yet loud and outspoken. I assumed that one day, someone would find my story, my words written on paper and find it to be so compelling that they would want to share. When I first began writing this story, my thoughts were solely that. I wrote this book in three days, less than seventy-two hours. I had yet another one of those unexplainable experiences, yet this one was not a dream, or a vision. It was an encounter. I know that a spirit, God perhaps, was in my bedroom that morning. When I heard the voice and as my bed shook, I was terrified. It had never happened like that before. The voice that I heard was not foreign, it was my dad, once again, just like the vision I had before. I knew it could not have been my dad in my bedroom, because at that moment, my dad had been gone for almost four years. I knew that it was God, coming to me in a familiar voice that I would recognize and accept. Though, on this journey of trying to find not only myself and figure out who I am, I was also on a journey trying to find God and figure out exactly who he was. I would often hear others speak of their encounters with God, and question why I had not been able to experience the same, I took them to be liars. God didn't happen like that, and if he did, what was so bad about me that he wasn't happening for me like that? I had not ever told anyone of my visions and dreams, because I didn't think anyone would understand me or it. I blamed God for giving me a gift that I could not open use comfortably, and one night with feelings of heavy doubt about what I was even doing, I simply stated to him, "You do not exist."

This particular morning, once my bed stopped shaking, I heard my dad's voice say, "I am here."

For some reason, I just knew that it was God. When I stood up erect like a statue up out of my bed, because I had been lying down after dropping my youngest daughter off at school, I immediately began bawling my eyes out. I was scared as all holy hell!

I called my pastor, because he was the only person I felt I could call and not have me admitted into the Psych ward at MUSC Hospital. I could not even speak when he answered the phone, I was so choked up that I began to hyperventilate. I could not get my words out; all I could do was sit on the phone and cry. He and my first lady patiently and quietly waited on the phone until I was able to finally get my words out. I didn't even know if anything that I was saying made any sense, because what had occurred truly didn't make any sense to me. Of all the questions that I had pertaining to God, religion, spirituality, all of the blame that I did, this was the moment of truth. The moment that I felt like God said, "Alright, time to quit allowing this one to play with my name, let me show her something."

One thing for sure, he never has to show me that ever again! I believe!

A few days after that encounter, I was again writing in my journal and having my personal bible study and the words "I blame God" fluttered out of my mouth and onto my journal pages. I then began to write down everything that I had blamed and was blaming God for. The first several lines were all bad things, but then as my list continued, they became less and less worse. By the time I had finished writing, I had seven pages, front and back, of blame. When I read over them, I saw growth as the list went on. Though, I know that I am nowhere near where I should be, I thank God that I am not where I used to be. I appreciate him for his patience. When I blamed him before for the bad, I now still blame him but for the good.

That job that I was praying to get would provide me with a clearer schedule, more money, and a better work culture. I blame God.

The peace within my home with the exclusion of toxic parenting. I blame God.

The sanity of my mind, restoring of my heart and peace that surpasses all my understanding. I blame God.

The gift of genuine friendships, full of love, laughter, and accountability. I blame God.

The love that is refreshing, patient, supportive, and invaluable. I blame God.

The children that are gifted and respectful. I blame God.

Life that has become worth living. I blame God.

I blame God for it all. The good and the bad, because without the bad, I would not be able to recognize and appreciate the good. He has given me a fresh new outtake on life and spirituality that I don't think I would have received had I not been honest with him and myself about where I truly was. I was appointed to write this book. The fact that it was written so thoroughly and so quickly further resonates with its purpose for me as to what this story will do for so many. I know that there are so many that have felt the things that I have felt within this book. There are some that blame God for many things, some that grew up in religious households, yet have no idea what God, church or spirituality even is. Some that just move along as they have been traditionally taught yet have no true feeling about God one way or another. I know there are many like this, because I was too, and if I am going to be completely honest, I still am. However, the direction I am moving forward in, desires to rid myself of those thoughts and insecurities when it comes to knowing him. I strive daily to be closer to him, know him more and be assured that he knows me too. I want to be able to have my name called from the book of life, I want to be told, servant well done, you may enter.

I had always been told by folks growing up and as an adult, that there was a calling on my life. I once confused that calling with being called into pulpit ministry, to follow in my mother's footsteps and become a preacher. I am so glad that I did not follow through with that, I probably would have been so miserable and denounce Christianity altogether. However, there are so many that are told that, yet they do not seek to find, nor do they wait to be directed into what that calling may be. It's true, we all do have a calling and a purpose. Many are out here walking into callings that do not belong to them, off the strength of what they were told by a prophet or holier than thou member of their family. That is why I said before, having discernment is a gift as well, that many do not possess. There are pulpit ministers that were called to be nothing more than an armor bearer. There are praise and worship leaders that were called to do nothing more than be a background singer or tambourine player. There are prophets and apostles laying hands and passing out certificates that were called to be nothing more than the minister of music. This is another topic for another day though, maybe for that other book I told you about that I may or may not write.

My blame to God was once my agony, now, it is my consolation. It is my reminder that I am not where I once was. It is a timeline into my grace and destiny. I do not regret blaming God for my past, it was because of those very bold statements towards the highest being that I demanded answer, direction, and solace from him as he promised he would provide. I applaud myself for even being courageous enough to sustain the backlash that would have come from such proclamations. I now relish the fact that he heard me, he came to see about me, and he is here with me, every step of the way.

Lately, every time I am in public, or see an old friend or acquaintance, the first thing that I am greeted with is, "Girl, you look so good.," that is not me. That is the glow of a peaceful life. That is the glow of overcoming. That is the glow of unwavering faith. That is the glow of sanity. That is the glow of new birth and restoration. That is the glow of what the comes with knowing God.

For those who read this, I am not trying to convert you. I am not one of those people who will preach down heaven and screaming "Say Jesus Jesus Jesus Jesus!" in your ear until you feel the move or the power. I am simply doing what I seem to do best, I'm writing. Those who are meant to be touched by the story will feel what they are intended to feel when they read it. Those who simply enjoy reading a good book will also do just that. My job is not to make you believe, only to tell you how I came to believe. My personal journey, one that I will remember, cherish, and hold near and dear to my heart until I am gone from this earth. I seek only to provide inspiration to those who seek to be inspired. My mom is the preacher, I am not. I am simply a good storyteller and can easily write about my life's occurrences in a way to provide you with your reading pleasure. I am here to only do as I was led to do. When you are given a task, God will not let you rest until that task is complete. It will come back to you over and over and over again. Though this book was written in a few short days, throughout the editing process, I continued to say, "Maybe I shouldn't release this book.," I continued to doubt the message between the pages, and what the readers would understand. However, God obviously has a much different plan. I don't know who this book may be meant to speak to, besides myself, but for whom ever will gain clarity, motivation, understanding and answers from the words on these pages, know that this is your confirmation from the man above, not from Desiree, I am merely the vessel.

As I continue my journey, because trust me, I haven't made it yet, I will only continue to blame God. I am blaming him for it all. I blame him for this new life, the refreshed glow, and the willingness to obey. I know that life will never be the same for me, not because everything is perfect, because it isn't, but mainly because my vision has changed. I have been given a new perspective, a new way to see the bigger picture. Things are becoming clearer, and my mind is not bogged or clouded. I am new. I am different. I am healed. I am restored. I am his.

I BLAME GOD!!!!

I Blame God

LET'S BLAME GOD TOGETHER

I have always loved journaling and writing, now here is your chance to do the same along with me.

When I wrote out my list of things that I blame God for, I was not expecting bad things to begin to turn to good things, but to be honest, I was angry with God.

But as I wrote, I realized that things were not so bad as they seemed. I want you to be very, very honest with yourself. If you feel struck, or like you are far away from God, trust me, he desires that closeness with you, and I know that you desire it with him.

Sit for a moment and think about all the things that you have experienced or may currently be experiencing in your life that you blame God for. ALL OF IT! Leave nothing out. Good things, mediocre things, and bad things! Make your list.

This is your petition to him, things that you may need answers on before you move forward. Make your list and then pray. Listen, don't do this if you are not ready for how you may receive the answers! I am not responsible for that part!

Let this be your release. Your "Trip to Greenville" per say. Empty your thoughts, put it all on paper. WRITE! Tell God what it is you want the answers to, Let's blame God together!

I pray he answers you.

I Blame God

Now, take a deep breath! Let it all out! Let's heal together!!!

I BLAME GOD!!!

Made in the USA
Columbia, SC
08 May 2024